CHRISTMAS IN SHAKESPEARE'S ENGLAND

'Bringing in the Boar's Head', an engraving from 1848, ILN.

CHRISTMAS IN SHAKESPEARE'S ENGLAND

Researched and compiled by

MARIA HUBERT

SUTTON PUBLISHING

First published in the United Kingdom in 1998
Sutton Publishing Limited · Phoenix Mill · Thrupp
Stroud · Gloucestershire · GL5 2BU

British Library Cataloguing in Publication Data
A catalogue record for this book is available from the British Library

ISBN 0-7509-1719-9

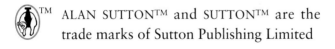

ALAN SUTTON™ and SUTTON™ are the
trade marks of Sutton Publishing Limited

Typeset in 11/15 Sabon.
Typesetting and origination by
Sutton Publishing Limited.
Printed in Great Britain by
Redwood Books Ltd, Trowbridge, Wiltshire.

CONTENTS

CONTENTS

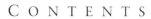

Shakespeare and Christmas

AN INTRODUCTION

Maria Hubert

William Shakespeare, we are told, was a gentle, fun-loving family man who worked hard for a living and was away from home and his wife, Anne Hathaway, more than he was with them. He dutifully visited home once a year, and spent quite a lot of time there while the plague devastated London. Thus the usual family orientated activities associated with the festive season, and which were actively endorsed as family pastimes by the queen herself, were not available to Will Shakespeare, and his wife and family had to make their Christmas entertainments without him.

Perhaps he would never have become a family man at all had it not been for the fact that Anne was already with child when they married in 1582, when Will was only eighteen years old. His writings portray him as a season-loving man, his May-ing songs and the bawdy frolics of some of his characters do not hint at austerity, and the restrictions of Puritanism were still far off. His Autolycus, in *The Winter's Tale*, frequented the fairs, wakes and bear-baiting shows with great glee, and mention is made of the puppet shows performing the mystery plays – many of which were Christmas plays. So why should such a person appear to be singularly lacking in Christmas spirit according to his critics? Here is one theory:

As a playwright popular with the nobility and royalty alike, Shakespeare was often in the final throes of a production in the weeks before Christmas. When most people, and indeed his own family, were preparing for the festive season, Will was directing his players, arranging the scenery (though he usually played on a bare stage it must be said, but that stage often needed to be safely erected within the palaces and halls he performed in) and costumes and making the last-minute changes to the performance, just as any director or playwright does today. It is very difficult to get into the spirit of the season when your best 'female' actor suddenly becomes a baritone; or an outbreak of some plague or fever knocks down the whole cast!

Certainly, throughout his sonnets can be seen the references to the summer as a carefree time, and the winter as dark, dismal and careworn.

> Or call it winter, which, being full of care,
> Makes summer's welcome thrice more wish'd, more rare

Of course, if his winters were filled with preparations for the Christmas enjoyment of others, then they were indeed 'full of care'.

As with his contemporaries, Shakespeare was in great demand during the festive season, and several of his plays were first performed during the traditional Twelve Days of Christmas. One of the most notable recorded was *Measure for Measure*, which is mentioned in the Christmas Revels Accounts for the Royal Court on 26 December 1604, as 'By His Majesties plaiers. On St. Stiuens [St Stephen's] night in the Hall. A play Called Mesure for Mesur, Shaxberd.' *The Plaie of Errors* by Shaxberd, *Love's Labour's Lost* and *King Lear*, were performed at the Court of James I during the Christmas season also.

And *Twelfth Night*, which by its title should contain many more references to the festive season than it does, was probably performed at the same court in about 1601–2 during the 'Revels' which generally began on Christmas Day and ended on Twelfth Night, or twelve days afterwards.

The Winter's Tale was also first performed before the Royal Court as part of the Christmas entertainments, and *Love's Labour's Lost*, which was an adaptation by Shakespeare of a much older story, was first performed by the Lord Chamberlain's Players, a company formed by the queen's cousin at her instigation, for Christmas 1597. Possibly there are others which I have missed, including *The Merry Wives of Windsor*, which, with the Bacchanalian character of Falstaff and the other characters and elements of the tale, lends itself so perfectly to the style of a Christmas masque that it is probable that the recorded performance before her Majesty Queen Elizabeth I might have been a Christmas showing. No wonder he did not get much of a Christmas himself! At a time when the queen was forcibly encouraging her lords and nobles back to their country seats to spend an old-fashioned Christmas with their families and tenants, Shakespeare must have found it a little hard at times.

Shakespeare presents his Christmas play to Queen Elizabeth I, from W. Sandy's Christmastide *(1830).*

Of all the Christmas verse written by his contemporaries, his is the least festive and least prolific. There is one poem which appears at the end of *Love's Labour's Lost*; the delightful 'Holly Song', both of which appear elsewhere in this anthology, and the most famously quoted verse from Hamlet,

> Some say that ever 'gainst that season comes,
> Wherein our Saviour's Birth is celebrated
> The bird of dawning singeth all night long:
> And then, they say, no spirit can walk abroad;
> The nights are wholesome; then no planets strike,
> No fairy takes, nor witch hath power to charm,
> So hallowed and so gracious is the time.

Shakespeare makes brief references to such seasonal delights as the game of Snapdragon in *Love's Labour's Lost* – which he calls 'Flap-dragon'. His comedy characters who, in both name and appearance, resemble the characters of the Christmas masques of both Henry VIII's and James I's reigns, notably Falstaff who appeared in *Henry IV* and *Henry V*, and was liked so much that the queen insisted that he appear again which is why Shakespeare put him into a comedy, *The Merry Wives of Windsor*.

His brief but striking comments on the season show him to be a man whose personal love of Christmas was at least equal to that of anyone in his time. The common customs of Christmas are mentioned as a casual matter and do not monopolize his works – even those written for a Christmas performance. After all, few Christmas productions are wholly about Christmas; even pantomime today tells a story which does not have a Christmas theme running through it, yet it is a Christmas tradition to the point of being an institution! Surely these Christmas performances of Shakespeare's could be seen as equal to pantomime.

The only contradiction to the concept of 'no Christmas content in a Christmas production', was *The Masque of Christmas* by Ben Jonson, a fellow playwright and friendly rival to Shakespeare. He, in fact, wrote the dedication of the first book of Shakespeare's complete works, which were published by friends of the Bard some seven years after his death. And, it must be said, this masque was the only masque written by Jonson which did have Christmas content as such.

It is probable that Shakespeare was just another hard-working man who was very busy over the festive season, and he had no time to sit contemplating the rime ice on the trees and write long poems about the frivolities of the season, as many of his poet contempories did.

The Christmas Entertainments

William Francis Dawson

Shakespeare was certainly born at a fortuitous time to succeed as a playwright. Queen Elizabeth I adored the play, and under her roof it grew to the height of importance. She kept singing boys, actors and

musicians, and formed several companies of players and theatrical performers. Shakespeare was commanded to write new plays for her court regularly, and she probably enjoyed the presence of this dashing and flamboyant character. The following description of the Queen's household players, and her contribution to theatrical entertainment, includes a charming anecdote about Shakespeare himself, and is from Dawson's Christmas and its Associations *(1903).*

The Christmas entertainments of Queen Elizabeth were enlivened by the beautiful singing of the children of her Majesty's Chapel. Queen Elizabeth I retained on her Royal establishment four sets of singing boys; which belonged to the Cathedral of St. Paul's; the Abbey of Westminster; St. George's Chapel Windsor and the Household Chapel. For the support and reinforcement of her musical bands, Elizabeth, like the other English Sovereigns, issued warrants for taking 'up suche apt and meete children, as are fitt to be instructed and framed in the Art and Science of Musicke and Singing.'

The children of the Chapel were also employed in the theatrical exhibitions represented at Court, for which their musical education had peculiarly qualified them. Richard Edwards, an eminent poet and musician of the 16th century, had written two comedies; 'Damon & Pythias' and 'Palemon & Arcite', which according to Wood, were often acted before the Queen, both at Court and at Oxford. With the latter of these the Queen was so delighted she promised Edwards a reward, which she subsequently gave him by making him first Gentleman of her Chapel, and in 1561 Master of the Children upon the death of Richard Bowyer.

As the Queen was particularly attached to dramatic entertainments, about 1569, she formed the children of the Royal Chapel into a company of theatrical performers, and placed them under the superintendence of Edwards. Not long after she formed a second society of players under the title, 'Children of the Revells' and by these two companies all Lyly's plays, and many of Shakespeare's and Jonson's were first performed. Ben Jonson has celebrated one of the chapel children, named Salathiel Pavy, who was famous for his performance of old men, but who died about 1601 aged thirteen.

The Shakespearean period had its grand Christmases, for The Christmas Players at the Court of Queen Elizabeth included England's greatest dramatist,

William Shakespeare; and the Queen not only took delight in witnessing Shakespeare's plays, but also admired the poet as a player. The histrionic ability of Shakespeare was by no means contemptible, though probably not such as to have transmitted his name to posterity had he confined himself exclusively to acting. Rowe informs us that, 'the tip-top of his performances was the ghost in his own Hamlet', Aubrey states that, 'He doth act exceedingly well' and Cheetle, a contemporary of the poet, who had seem him perform, assures us that, 'he was excellent in the quality that he professed'.

An anecdote is preserved in connection with Shakespeare's playing before Queen Elizabeth I. While he was taking the part of a king, Elizabeth rose, and, in crossing the stage, dropped her glove as she passed the poet. No notice was taken by him of the incident; and the queen, desirous of finding out whether this was the result of inadvertence, or a determination to preserve the consistency of his part, moved again towards him, and again dropped her glove. Shakespeare then stooped down to pick it up, saying, in the character of the monarch whom he was playing 'And though now bent on this high embassy/ Yet stoop we to take up our cousin's glove'.

He then retired and presented the glove to the Queen, who was highly pleased with his courtly performance.

Tribute by Digression

T h o m a s   H e r v e y

Shakespeare knew how to appeal to the tastes of the great Queen Elizabeth I, a skill noted, but possibly misinterpreted, by the historian of popular antiquities, Thomas Hervey, writing in the late eighteenth and early nineteenth centuries. Hervey specialized in Christmas, and was one of the great scholars who researched and recorded the ancient customs before they died away in the later Georgian reigns. His history of Christmas was, and possibly still is, second to none, but in the course of discussing the festivities of an Elizabethan Christmas, he is desperately sidetracked in his total adulation of the great Bard! The

*points he makes are most valid, the manner in which he writes is
cringingly comical at times. (The following text is adapted and abridged
from the original which is too flowery and opinionated for our purposes,
but readers may find it in Hervey's* Booke of Christmasse *[1833].)*

Our readers, we think, need scarcely be told that the successor to this stern and miserable queen (Queen Mary) was sure to seize upon the old pageantries. . . . From all the old altars which the court had reared to old Father Christmas of yore, a cloud of incense was poured into the royal closet enough to choke anything but the Tudor queen. The festival was saved, and even embellished; but the saint, as far as the court was concerned, was changed. However, the example of the festivity to the people was the same; and the land was a merry land, and the Christmas time a merry time, throughout its length and breadth in the time of Queen Elizabeth.

Under these impulses, the old dramatic entertainments took a higher character and assumed a more consistent form. The first regular English tragedy, called 'Ferrex and Porrex' and the entertainment of 'Gammer Gurton's Needle' were both productions of the early period of the Queen's reign:– and amid the crowd of her worshippers rose up – with the star upon his forehead which will burn there for all time, – the very first of all created beings, William Shakespeare. These are among the strange anomalies which the world, as it is constituted, so often presents; and must present at times, constitute it how we will. – Shakespeare doing homage to Queen Elizabeth I! – The loftiest genius and the noblest heart that have yet walked this earth, in a character merely human, bowing down before this woman, with the soul of a milliner, and no heart at all! – The swayer of hearts, the ruler of men's minds, in virtue of his own transcendent nature, recognising the supremacy of this overgrown child, because she presided over the temporalities of a half emancipated nation.

To any who will amuse himself by looking over the miracle plays and masques which were replaced by the more regular forms of dramatic entertainment, and will then regale himself by the perusal of the two plays already mentioned, which came forward with higher pretentions in the beginning of this reign, there will appear reason to be sufficiently astonished at the rapid strides by which dramatic excellence was attained before its close, and during the next reign, even without taking Shakespeare into account at all.

But when we turn to the marvels of this great magician, and find that, in his hands, not only were the forms of the drama perfected, but that, – without impeding the action or interest invested in those forms, and despite his excursions into the regions of imagination and his creations out of the natural world, – he has touched every branch of human knowledge and struck into every train of human thought, that, without learning, in the popular sense, he has arrived at all the results, and embodied all the wisdom, which learning is only useful if it teaches. We can be placed in no imaginable circumstances, and under the influence of no possible feelings, of which we do not find exponents on his page, and above all, when we find that all the final morals to be drawn from his writings are hopeful ones, – that all the lessons which are his agents – joy or sorrow, pain or pleasure, are made alike to teach, are lessons of goodness, and it is impossible to attribute all this to aught but a revelation, or ascribe to him any character but that of a prophet.

Shakespeare knew more than any other mere man ever knew; and none can tell how that knowledge came to him. 'All men's business and bosoms' lay open to him. We should not like to have him quoted against us on any subject. Nothing escaped him, and he never made a mistake (we are not speaking of technical ones). He was the universal interpreter into any language of the human mind; and he knew all the myriad voices by which nature speaks. He reminds us of the Vizier in the Eastern story, who is said to understand the language of all animals. The uttering of the elements, the voices of the beasts and of birds, Shakespeare could translate into the language of men; and the thoughts and sentiments of men he rendered into words as sweet as the singing of birds.

But we are digressing – and who does not, when the image of Shakespeare comes across him?!

Elizabethan Christmas

M i c h a e l   H a r r i s o n

Through her love of theatrical entertainment, Queen Elizabeth I gave patronage and credence to the stage in the late sixteenth and early seventeenth centuries. It might be said that thanks to her William

Shakespeare, and the many who followed his example, are so well known today. She acceded to the throne of England just seven years before Shakespeare was born and so he grew up in an England both tolerant and favourable towards those with theatrical leanings. Drama had become fashionable. No longer the entertainment of the street, plays and pageants were now elevated to the Royal Court and noble houses.
Michael Harrison wrote extensively on traditional and historical customs in the 1950s. The following extract is from the Tatler *magazine in 1951, which aptly describes a Christmas at the Court of Queen Elizabeth, with a particular emphasis on the evolution of theatrical entertainment and the stage under Elizabeth's patronage, from which Shakespeare would have benefited, having spent many Christmases at Queen Elizabeth's court producing plays for her.*

On November 17th (old style) Elizabeth succeeded to the throne on the death of her elder sister Mary, and Elizabeth's first Christmas as Queen was spent in making preparations for the Coronation, which had been fixed for January 15th following.

Elizabeth's differences with her sister are too well known not to mention here; it is necessary only to state that those differences did not include any difference on the subject of the respect which ought to be paid to Christmas except that Elizabeth's were gayer, more magnificent and generally much more costly than those of Mary's reign.

Elizabeth inherited all her father's liking for boisterous pleasures, as witness this extract from a letter, written in 1572, by Christopher Playter to Mr. Kytson, of Hengrove Hall:

'At Chris-time here were certayne masters of defence, that did challenge all comers at all weapons, as long-sworde, staff, sword and buckler, rapier with the dagger: and here were many broken heads, and one of the masters of defence dyed upon the hurt which he received on the head. The challenge was before the quenes Majestie who seemes to have pleasure therein; for when some of them would have sollen a broken pate, her Majesty bade him not to be ashamed to put off his cap, and the blood was spied to run about his face. There was also at the corte new plays which lasted almost all night. The name of the play was huff, suff and ruff, with other masks both of ladies and gents.'

The mention of 'masks' reminds us that it was in Elizabeth's reign that the older pageant – 'enterludes' or 'disgysings' they had been called – turned into

*Typical courtyard theatre playing
Shakespeare's* A Midsummer Night's Dream,
from Cassell's Illustrated History *(N.D.).*

the masque: that is to say, plot was added to the mere spectacle which had pleased an earlier age.

It was at a Christmas Feast of Philip and Mary that the first English comedy ever to be performed was acted; and it was at the Inner Temple's 'Grand Christmas' of 1561–62, that the first English tragedy, *Gorboduc*, written by two young members of the Bar, was first played. Elizabeth loved, as did her father, rough and tumble entertainments; if with broken pates and some obvious blood, so much the better; but she was a patroness, at once enthusiastic and admirably competent, of the stage. Theatrical entertainments were a constant source of pleasure to the queen, and it was she herself who, by organizing the presentation of plays, brought the modern stage into being.

In 1569 she formed the Children of the Chapel Royal into a theatrical company under the personal control of Richard Edwards, poet, musician and playwright; and soon after, Elizabeth formed a second company, the Children of the Revels, whose 'star' – immortalized in the beautiful epitaph that Ben Jonson wrote – was a child actor named Salathiel Pavy, who died at the age of thirteen.

These Children of the Revels performed plays by the age's leading writers among them Lyly, Ben Jonson and Shakespeare – and there is a story that Shakespeare himself acted in his own plays, before the Queen.

But the coming of the modern type of stage play, did not, for many years, send the older pageants out of fashion; and the 'masque' with the scripts by Ben Jonson, and 'sets' by Inigo Jones was to come to a period of costly splendour before being killed by the Commonwealth.

In the reign of Elizabeth, England made the decisive change-over from pastoral to being a commercial nation; and the change-over made two classes very powerful – the lawyers and the merchants – so that the Inns of

Court and the City's Livery Companies quickly came to be in a position to rival the Crown as patrons of the arts and givers of splendid entertainments, especially at Christmastime.

The Inns of Court were the especial upholders of that curious institution, the Lord of Misrule, though to be sure, he was not neglected by the colleges of the two universities. The Inner Temple, besides appointing a Lord of Misrule to preside over its Christmas junketings ('A repast at dinner is 8*d*'), used to invite some person of great distinction to be the Constable-Marshall for the days of Christmas; and Robert Dudley, afterwards Earl of Leicester, was honoured to accept the appointment of Constable-Marshall for the Christmas of 1561–2. On Boxing Day – then known as St Stephen's Day – he presented himself in Inner Temple hall, 'in gilt armour, with a nest of feathers of all colours on his helm, and a gilt pole-axe in his hand; with him, sixteen trumpeters, four drum and fife, and four men armed from the middle upwards'.

All the sonorous ritual of medieval pageantry was called upon to make these functions as impressive as possible; and to read the Order of Service for the Inner Temple Christmas of that year in which Dudley was Constable-Marshall is to realize how far we have progressed on the road to universal and total drabness!

All 'persons of worship', especially Lieutenants and Sheriffs of counties, kept their Lords of Misrule; and though the Puritans thundered against the custom, even the common people seem to have elected their Christmas Princes or Lords of Misrule; for Parkhurst, Bishop of Norwich, had to issue an injunction in the following terms:

'Item, that no person or persons call themselves lords of misrule in the Christmas tyme, or other vnreuerent* persons at any other tyme, presume to come into church vnreuerently* playing their lewd partes, with scoffing, jesting or ribaldry talke, and if any haue alredy offended herein, to present their names to the ordinery.'

Three persons who were unwise enough to act the parts as bride, bridegroom and parson at a Christmas mock-marriage were sent to repent of their folly in the stocks.

The favourite pastimes of the Queen were dancing and dicing: her luck at the latter being constantly assured by the prudent use of a loaded dice!

---

* irreverent

National calamities and acts of God – and there were many in Elizabeth's reign – were never considered sufficient reasons, or, indeed, reasons at all, for the Queen's not keeping Christmas, either at Hampton Court, Greenwich or Nonsuch, in royal state.

'The plague', writes Lord Shrewsbury to his Lady in 1568, 'is disposed far abrode in London. So that the Queen kepes hur Kyrsomas her, and goth not to Grenwych, as it was mete.' ('Her' being Hampton Court).

'If ye would,' wrote Sir Thomas Smith from Hampton Court, Christmas 1572, 'what we do here we play at tables, dance and keep Christmas'.

Some of the entertainments of the time strike us in this age as being unnecessarily rough. After the elaborate ritual of St Stephen's Day was ended in the Inner Temple, with the Constable-Marshalls having presided over various ceremonies, 'the Master of the Game standeth up'.

'This ceremony also performed, a Huntsman cometh into the Hall, with a fox and a purse-net; with a cat, both bound at the end of a staff . . .'.

It goes on to describe a stomach churning spectacle, and ends with, 'and then proceedeth the second course'! How any of the guests could eat after such 'sport' one cannot, today, imagine.

Elizabethan Master of Revels.

Queen Elizabeth's Master of Revels was for many years, Sir Thomas Cawarden; and it was he who superintended the plays and pageants of Elizabeth's first Royal Christmas. An 'economy drive' being ordered by the Queen, Sir Thomas managed to reduce the expenses to £227 11 shillings – £220 less than had been spent the previous Christmas; but these figures were not to remain long at this low level. With the increasing wealth that trade was to bring, the cost of the Christmas entertainments was to be increased at least a hundred times by the beginning of the following reign.

If there is a point at which the Elizabethan Christmas was different from our own it is to be found in the absence of what we might call the 'private' Christmas. All Christmas entertainments were then given for as many persons as possible; and as the poor depended on the Christmas largesse of the noblemen and country gentlemen, Elizabeth passed an act sending the owners back to their estates at Christmas, so that the traditional Christmas entertainment of their tenants should not be allowed to go by default through the absenteeism of their landlords.

Nichols, in his 'Progresses of Queen Elizabeth' tells how, on Twelfth Day, the Lord Mayor, aldermen and all the Crafts of London, and the Batchelors of the Mayors Company, went in procession to St Paul's, 'after the old custom', and there heard a sermon. The same day a stage was set up for a play; and after the play was over a fine 'mask', and afterwards a great banquet which lasted till midnight.

The new rich were building their splendid palaces all over England, designed by such architects as John Thorpe and 'John the Italian' Wilton, Hatfield, Cobham Hall, Penshurst and many other famous houses all dating from this time, and these noble mansions were the scenes of the richest and most elaborate entertainments, especially after Elizabeth had ordered their owners to keep Christmas at home; Ben Jonson has left on record how nobly he was entertained at Penshurst.

Eating was on a grand scale – as it was to remain for nearly four centuries afterwards; and the food was cheap for the poor, so that Christmas was celebrated lavishly by all classes. The Christmas Pudding had not yet made its appearance in history, but its predecessor, plum porridge – a sort of soup made from bread, raisins, sherry, meat, suet, various spices and coloured with saffron – was universally eaten as a ritual dish.

All the same, there had been a marked tendency to simplify the cooking. Boars' Heads, elaborately decorated, were still the *pièce de résistance* of the Christmas Board, but we hear no more of the 'peacock endored' and the other 'subtleties' which were such a feature of the medieval banquet.

Food becomes simpler as its variety increases. There were changes too in the drinking habits of the nation. The art of distilling spirits is supposed to have been invented by the Arabs in the 13th century, and by the end of the 15th century the manufacture of Brandy had become widespread in the wine producing countries. But it was not until the reign of Elizabeth that the use of spirits became general in Britain, and according to Campden, the English

Putting up the holly bough (Frank Merrill, 1895).

troops serving in the Low Countries did much towards introducing the practice in England.

Possibly the bad condition of the Ale may have been respons-ible for the avidity in which drinkers turned to brandy.

The accent was on good eating and drinking in the days of Good Queen Bess. Elizabeth was much more an autocrat than a bigot; and the acts by which earlier monarchs had sought to forbid card-playing to the lower orders was not found in her reign. She – like all the Tudors – loved card playing, as all other forms of gambling; but she saw no reason to forbid these pleasures to lesser folk. The age then, saw a tremendous rise in the use of playing cards, dicing and other pastimes.

The Christmas Tree had not yet been introduced from Germany. But at Christmas, during Elizabethan times, holly and ivy and other evergreens were hung everywhere. A particular pleasant custom was wreathing of the public monuments in greenery during the days of Christmas.

And that those Elizabethan Christmases were 'merry', there can be no doubt; for the Queen did not think it unworthy of her notice to prevent rises in the cost of those material comforts upon which much of the merriness of Christmas depended.

When in 1591, the powerful Brewers Company sent in a remonstrance against their being compelled to sell beer at a price fixed six years earlier, although every material employed in brewing had greatly increased in price, Elizabeth rejected their protest; and compelled them to withdraw the increased prices that they had taken upon themselves to charge.

The Elizabethans had no 'proprietary' whisky, no cigarettes, no Christmas cards or trees, no coffee, tea or television; but there's no doubt that they had all the ingredients for a right merry Christmas – and of those ingredients they followed the example of their great queen, they made full use of.

'Winter' from Love's Labour's Lost

William Shakespeare

Shakespeare's 'Winter's Song' appears at the end of Love's Labour's Lost *and was originally sung by a group of the players, coming on stage at the end of this Christmas performance. It was first performed for Queen Elizabeth in 1597 and first published in the Quarto edition in 1598 with the following legend: 'A Pleasant Conceited Comedie Love's labors lost. As it was presented before her Highness this last Christmas. Newly corrected and augmented By William Shakespeare', though one is inclined to look to an earlier edition if indeed this one was 'newly corrected' as it states.*

The principal singers are introduced, 'This side is Heims, Winter – this Ver, Spring; the one maintained by the owl, the other by the cuckoo. Ver begin.' The first part is sung by Spring, with her chorus Cuckoo; the part of

'Tom bears logs into the hall'. An engraving depicting Shakespeare's 'Winter Song', from Christmas with the Poets *by the Vitzelly Brothers (1840).*

'Winter's Song' which we reproduce here is sung by Winter with her Owl in full voice. The song bears no reference to the play content, which is full of topical innuendos which obviously meant something more to the audience at Queen Elizabeth's court than they do to the modern reader. But it is clear that this ending was added purely for the Christmas season, just as one would find a few 'Christmassy' songs in a modern pantomime.

The following copy is reproduced not from that Quarto edition, but from a book published in 1840, with its charming little tribute to the Bard: 'The "Winter Song" from Shakespeare's Love's Labour's Lost, *furnishes us with a picture in every line, and leaves us cause for regret that the few poems that we have here collected together, comprise the whole that the poet of all time has written relative to our subject:'*

'Then nightly sings the staring owl', from Christmas with the Poets *by the Vitzelly Brothers (1840).*

When icicles hang by the wall,
And Dick, the Shepherd blows his nail,
And Tom bears logs into the hall,
And milk comes frozen home in pail;

When blood is nipped, and ways be foul,
Then nightly sings the staring owl,
To-whoo;
Tu-whit, to-whoo, a merry note,
While greasy Joan doth keel* the pot

When all aloud the wind doth blow,
And coughing, drowns the parson's saw,
And birds sit brooding in the snow,
A Marian's nose looks red and raw.

When roasted crabs hiss in the bowl,
Then nightly sings the staring owl,
To-whoo;
Tu-whit, to-whoo, a merry note,
While greasy Joan doth keel* the pot.

* cool

Roasted Crabs & Wassails

WITH 'CAROL FOR THE WASSAIL BOWL'

From *Christmas with the Poets by the Vitzelly Brothers*

In Shakespeare's 'Winter Song', he speaks of the 'Roasted Crabs
hissing in the bowl'. The Crabs were little bright red apples, which were
grown for their sharp taste when added to other foods, and the high
pectin, which was used for preserving and jelling. Their chief use at
Christmastide was as an ingredient for the Wassail Bowl. When roasted,
they split open to reveal a fluffy whiteness, which spooned on to the
spiced ale or cider was called 'Lamb's wool'.

Many ceremonies and traditions were observed. The Wassailers,
however poor, had to be welcomed into the house no matter how grand.
To refuse them was refusing the good fortune they brought.
(Christianity, as well as more ancient custom, also taught that this was
the season to give alms to the poor for the cleansing of one's own life or
soul.) A few verses were sung before admittance, then the following
verses were full of well-wishing and blessings upon the household,
ending with a request for alms, which were never refused or
they took their good fortune away with them. This was a
time of much superstition, and few would take the risk of
losing their fortune!

Neither should they refuse to drink from the proffered bowl. The
original Wassail is said to have come from a much older custom,
whereby enmity was broken and peace signed by the drinking of the
Peace Cup – an ale drink. The phrase 'Wassail' comes from the Saxon,
'Wachs Heil', meaning 'I give you health'.

Here is an extract from a piece about the Wassail Bowl, followed
by a Wassail song, which may even have been sung at Shakespeare's
own front door – it would be certainly most unlikely that he

'The Wassailers'. An engraving by Birket Foster, 1853.

did not know this famous old drinking song, which was sung by groups of maidens carrying around their bowl from house to house over the festive season.

The Boar's Head and the Wassail Bowl were the two most important accessories to Christmas in the olden times, and there are frequent allusions to the latter in the works of our early English poets. The word 'Wassail' occurs in the oldest carol that has been handed down to us, and in extracts from Spenser, Shakespeare and Ben Jonson mention is made of the Wassail Bowl, which shows that in their day, it continued to form a necessary portion of the festivities belonging to the Christmas season. New Year's Eve and

*Twelfth Night were the occasions on which the Wassail Bowl was
chiefly in requisition . . .*

*While the wealthier classes were enjoying themselves with
copious draughts of 'Lamb's wool' – as the beverage, composed of
ale, nutmeg, sugar, toast and roasted crabs or apples, with which
the bowl was filled, was styled – the poorer people went from
house to house with Wassail Bowls adorned with ribbons, singing
carols, and inviting those they visited to drink, in return for
which little presents of money were generally bestowed
upon them.*

A CAROL FOR THE WASSAIL BOWL

A Jolly Wassail Bowl
A Wassail of good ale,
Well fare the butler's soul,
That setteth this to sale –
Our Jolly Wassail.

Good Dame, here at your door
Our Wassail we begin,
We are all maidens poor,
We now pray let us in,
With our Wassail.

Our Wassail we do fill
With apples and with spice,
Then grant us your good will,
To taste here once or twice
Of our Wassail

If any maidens be
Here dwelling in this house,
They kindly will agree
To take a full carouse
Of our Wassail.

But here they let us stand
All freezing in the cold;
Good Master, give command
To enter and be bold,
With our Wassail.

*Once admitted the Wassailers
continue thus:*

Much joy into this hall
With us is entered in,
Our Master first of all,
We hope will now begin,
Of our Wassail.

And after, his good Wife
Our spiced bowl will try, –
The Lord prolong your life!
Good fortune we espy,
For our Wassail.

Some Bounty from your hands,
Our Wassail to maintain:
We'll buy no house nor lands
With which we do gain,
With our Wassail.

This is our merry night
Of choosing King and Queen
Then let it be your delight
That something may be seen
In our Wassail.

After the alms have been given:

It is a noble part,
To bear a liberal mind;
God Bless our Master's heart!
For here we comfort find,
With our Wassail.

And now we must be gone,
To seek out more good cheer;
Where bounty will be shown,
As we have found it here.
With our Wassail.

As they leave:

Much joy betide them all,
Our prayers shall be still,
We hope, and ever shall,
For this, your great goodwill
To our Wassail.

My Lorde of Misserule

from The Anatomie of Abuses *by*
Philip Stubbs

*This paper was a rather cynical description of festivals and frivolities
of the sixteenth century, giving an accurate if somewhat jaundiced view
of the customs of the times. The following describes the 'king' of
Twelfth Night, called the Lord of Misrule, whose task it was
to 'rule' over the festivities for the duration of the party. There were
many ways of electing a king; some chose a card, others picked
a piece of cake which had a bean in it, others were elected
by popular vote. He would then choose a 'court' of followers, who*

*would do his bidding and adopt silly names and titles. He could be
a sensible king, who made sure that the party did not get too out of
hand, or he could be quite Bacchanalian, ordering people to do silly
things. Some did actually try to attend Church services in this way. They
were usually stopped by the clergy, who often hired 'heavies' for the
occasion! But those who were powerful enough could not be stopped. In
the following description they sound like morris men
in fact, although the early mummers and masquers who visited house to
house were similar. This is a typical case of three distinct customs
becoming combined.*

Firste all the wilde heades of the parishe conventynge together, chuse
them a grand Capitaine (of mischeef) whom they innoble with the title
of my Lorde of Misserule, and hym they crown with great solemnitie, and
adopt for their kyng. This kyng anoynted, chuseth for the twentie, fourtie,
three score or a hundred lustie guttes like to hymself, to waite uppon his
lordely majestie, and to guard his noble persone. Then every one of these his
menne he investeth with his liveries of greene, yellowe or some other light
wanton colour. And as though that were not

baudie enough I should saie, they bedecke
themselves with scarffes, ribons, and laces,
hanged all over with golde rynges, precious
stones, and other jewelles: this doen, they
tye about either legge twentie or fourtie
belles with rich handkercheefs in their
handes, and sometymes laid acrosse over
their shoulders and neckes, borrowed for
the moste parte of their pretie Mopsies
and loovying Bessies, for bussyng them in
the darcke.

Thus thinges sette in order, they have
their hobbie horses, dragons, and other
antiques, together with their baudie
pipers, and thunderyng drommers, to
strike up the Deville's Daunce withall, and
marche these heathen companie towardes
the church and churche yarde, their pipers piping,

drommers thonderyng, their stumppes dauncyng, their belles iynglyng, their handkerchiefes swyngyng about their heades like madmen, their hobbie horses and other monsters skyrmishyng amongst the throng: and in this sorte they goe to the churche (though the minister bee at praier or preechyng) dauncyng and swingyng their handkercheefes over their heades, in the churche, like devilles incarnate, with suche a confused noise that no man can heare his owne voice. Then the foolishe people, they looke, they stare, they laugh, they fleere, and mount upon formes and pewes, to see these goodly pageauntes, solemnized in this sort.

Love's Labour's Lost

William Shakespeare, with an introduction by Maria Hubert

No anthology of Shakespeare would be complete without an extract from one of his works. Unfortunately, not one of his plays was about Christmas, but many were written specifically to be performed during the Christmas season and usually before Queen Elizabeth and her Court. His Comedies were most popular.

Love's Labour's Lost is an elegant play. The story was an old one, in existence long before Shakespeare produced his version of it, but obscure until his genius brought it to the forefront of theatre and literature.

It was originally performed by the Lord Chamberlain's Players. This Company was formed, at the Queen's instigation, by her cousin, the Lord Chamberlain. Companies which were not afforded a Royal approval were frowned upon, so it was fortunate that the Queen enjoyed play-acting so much that she approved a number of such companies to play before her. These companies took their names from the patrons who founded and sponsored them; thus the popular groups were such as The Lord Admiral's Men, My Lord Pembroke's Men, etc.

Shakespeare, together with James Burbage and James's two sons, Richard and Cuthbert, who were old friends of Shakespeare from his earlier years as an actor, all bought a shareholding into the Lord Chamberlain's Players. The four were firm friends who continued to write and produce together for some thirty years.

Love's Labour's Lost was reported to have been Queen Elizabeth's favourite. He produced it for her as part of the Christmas Revells in 1597, and in 1598 it was published by Cuthbert Burbage as 'A Pleasant conceited Comedie called Love's Labour's Lost. As it was presented before her Highness this last Christmas.'

The story is set in Navarre in Spain, but, other than that, the play is in no way Spanish. It is a fashionable play, incorporating the popular themes and fashionable styles of thought, writing and communication of the day. The language is courtly and flowery, and was obviously designed to impress the Royal Court rather than the average playgoer of the time.

The gentlemen of the King of Navarre's Court (in the play) decide that they should, in order to better themselves spiritually and in all things knowledgeable, retire from the world of women for three years and dedicate themselves to learning and contemplation. However, their highbrow ideals fall flat as one by one they all fall in love and contrive to meet or communicate with their ladyloves. They send them gifts, pearls, a book and poetry.

We take up the story in Act V, sc. ii, as the King and his three lovesick lords decide to disguise themselves as Russians and visit their ladies undetected. The ladies discover the plan and decide to disguise themselves with masks and change their gifts around to confuse their lovers so they will woo the wrong girl. Here the story becomes a very sophisticated farce, with many other elements thrown in for good measure. Finally, having had their fun, the ladies admit that they knew all along, to the embarrassment and chagrin of their lords. Biron retorts: 'I see the trick o'nt – Here was a consent, Knowing aforehand of our merriment, To dash it like a Christmas Comedy.'

Enter the King, Biron, Longaville and Dumain, in Russian habits and masked; Moth, musicians and attendants:

Moth.   All hail the richest beauties on the earth!
Boyet.   Beauties no richer than rich taffeta.
Moth.   A holy parcel of the fairest dames!
                    [*The ladies turn their backs to him.*

	That ever turn'd their – backs – to mortal views!
Biron.	Their eyes, villain, their eyes.
Moth.	That ever turn'd their eyes to mortal views!
	Out –
Boyet.	True; out indeed.
Moth.	Out of your favours, heavenly spirits vouchsafe
	Not to behold –
Biron.	Once to behold, rogue.
Moth.	Once to behold with your sun-beamed eyes, – with your sun-beamed eyes –
Boyet.	They will not answer to that epithet; You were best call it daughter-beamed eyes.
Moth.	They do not mark me, and that brings me out.
Biron.	Is this your perfectness? be gone, you rogue. [*Exit Moth.*
Ros.	What would these strangers? Know their minds, Boyet:
	If they do speak our language, 'tis our will
	That some plain man recount our purposes:
	Know what they would.
Boyet.	What would you with the princess?
Biron.	Nothing but peace and gentle visitation.
Ros.	What would they, say they?
Boyet.	Nothing but peace and gentle visitation.
Ros.	Why, that they have; and bid them so be gone.
Boyet.	She says you have it, and you may be gone.
King.	Say to her we have measured many miles
	To tread a measure with her on this grass.
Boyet.	They say that they have measured many a mile.
	To tread a measure with you on this grass.
Ros.	It is not so. Ask them how many inches
	Is in one mile: if they have measur'd many,
	The measure, then, of one is easily told.
Boyet.	If to come hither you have measur'd miles,
	And many miles, the princess bids you tell
	How many inches do fill up one mile.
Biron.	Tell her we measure them by weary steps.
Boyet.	She hears herself.
Ros.	How many weary steps,

	Of the many weary miles you have o'ergone,
	Are number'd in the travel of one mile?
Biron.	We number nothing that we spend for you;
	Our duty is so rich, so infinite,
	That we may do it still without accompt.
	Vouchsafe to show the sunshine of your face,
	That we, like savages, may worship it.
Ros.	My face is but a moon, and clouded too.
King.	Blessed are clouds, to do as such clouds do!
	Vouchsafe, bright moon, and these thy stars, to shine, –
	Those clouds removed, – upon our wat'ry eyne.
Ros.	O vain petitioner! beg a greater matter;
	Thou now request'st but moonshine in the water.
King.	Then, in our measure do but vouchsafe one change:
	Thou bid'st me beg; this begging is not strange.
Ros.	Play music, then: nay, you must do it soon. [*Music plays.*
	Not yet; – no dance: – thus change I like the moon.
King.	Will you not dance? How come you thus estrang'd?
Ros.	You took the moon at full; but now she's chang'd.
King.	Yet still she is the moon and I the man.
	The music plays; vouchsafe some motion to it.
Ros.	Our ears vouchsafe it.
King.	But your legs should do it.
Ros.	Since you are strangers, and come here by chance,
	We'll not be nice; take hands; – we will not dance.
King.	Why take we hands, then?
Ros.	Only to part friends; –
	Court'sy sweet hearts; and so the measure ends.
King.	More measure of this measure; be not nice.
Ros.	We can afford no more at such a price.
King.	Prize you yourselves: what buys your company?
Ros.	Your absence only.
King.	That can never be.
Ros.	Then cannot we be bought: and so adieu;
	Twice to your visor and half once to you!
King.	If you deny to dance, let's hold more chat.
Ros.	In private then.

King.	I am best pleas'd with that.
	[They converse apart.
Biron.	White-handed mistress, one sweet word with thee.
Prin.	Honey, and milk, and sugar; there is three.
Biron.	Nay, then, two treys, – an if you grow so nice, –
	Metheglin, wort, and malmsey; – well run, dice!
	There's half a dozen sweets.
Prin.	Seventh sweet adieu!
	Since you can cog, I'll play no more with you.
Biron.	One word in secret.
Prin.	Let it not be sweet.
Biron.	Thou griev'st my gall.
Prin.	Gall? bitter.
Biron.	Therefore meet.
	[They converse apart.
Dum.	Will you vouchsafe with me to change a word?
Mar.	Name it.
Dum.	Fair lady, –
Mar.	Say you so? Fair lord, –
	Take that for your fair lady.
Dum.	Please it you,
	As much in private, and I'll bid adieu.
	[They converse apart.
Kath.	What, was your visard made without a tongue?
Long.	I know the reason, lady, why you ask.
Kath.	O for your reason! quickly, sir; I long.
Long.	You have a double tongue within your mask,
	And would afford my speechless visard half.
Kath.	Veal, quoth the Dutchman; – is not veal a calf?
Long.	A calf, fair lady!
Kath.	No, a fair lord calf.
Long.	Let's part the word.
Kath.	No, I'll not be your half:
	Take all, and wean it; it may prove an ox.
Long.	Look how you butt yourself in these sharp mocks!
	Will you give horns, chaste lady? do not so.
Kath.	Then die a calf, before your horns do grow.

Long.   One word in private with you ere I die.

Kath.   Bleat softly, then; the butcher hears you cry.

                 [*They converse apart.*

Boyet.   The tongues of mocking wenches are as keen

          As is the razor's edge invisible,

          Cutting a smaller hair than may be seen;

          Above the sense of sense; so sensible

          Seemeth their conference; their conceits have wings.

          Fleeter than arrows, bullets, wind, thought, swifter things.

Ros.   Not one word more, my maids; break off, break off.

Biron.   By heaven, all dry-beaten with pure scoff!

King.   Farewell, mad wenches; you have simple wits.

         [*Exeunt King, Lords, Music, and Attendants.*

Prin.   Twenty adieus, my frozen Muscovites, –

          Are these the breed of wits so wonder'd at?

Boyet.   Tapers they are, with your sweet breaths puffed out.

Ros.   Well-liking wits they have; gross, gross; fat, fat.

Prin.   O poverty in wit, kingly-poor flout!

          Will they not, think you, hang themselves tonight?

          Or ever, but in visards, show their faces?

          This pert Biron was out of countenance quite.

Ros.   O, they were all in lamentable cases!

          The king was weeping-ripe for a good word.

Prin.   Biron did swear himself out of all suit.

Mar.   Dumain was at my service, and his sword:

          No point, quoth I; my servant straight was mute.

Kath.   Lord Longaville said I came o'er his heart;

          And trow you what he called me?

Prin.   Qualm, perhaps.

Kath.   Yes in good faith.

Prin.   Go, sickness as thou art!

Ros.   Well, better wits have worn plain statue-caps.

          But will you hear? the king is my love sworn.

Prin.   And quick Biron hath plighted faith to me.

Kath.   And Longaville was for my service born.

Mar.   Dumain is mine, as sure as bark on tree.

Boyet.   Madam, and pretty mistresses, give ear:

	Immediately they will again be here
	In their own shapes; for it can never be
	They will digest this harsh indignity.
Prin.	Will they return?
Boyet.	They will, they will, God knows,
	And leap for joy, though they are lame with blowes;
	Therefore, change favours; and, when they repair,
	Blow like sweet roses in this summer air.
Prin.	How blow? how blow? speak to be understood.
Boyet.	Fair ladies mask'd are roses in their bud:
	Dismask'd, their damask sweet commixture shown,
	Are angels vailing clouds, or roses blown.
Prin.	Avaunt, perplexity! What shall we do
	If they return in their own shapes to woo?
Ros.	Good madam, if by me you'll be advis'd,
	Let's mock them still, as well known as disguis'd:
	Let us complain to them what fools were here,
	Disguis'd like Muscovites, in shapeless gear;
	And wonder what they were, and to what end
	Their shallow shows and prologue vilely penn'd,
	And their rough carriage so ridiculous,
	Should be presented at our tent to us.
Boyet.	Ladies, withdraw; the gallants are at hand.
Prin.	Whip to our tents, as roes run over land.

                                             [Exeunt Prin., Ros., Kath., and Mar.

Re-enter the King, Biron, Longaville, and Dumain, in their proper habits.

King.	Fair sir, God save you! Where is the princess?
Boyet.	Gone to her tent. Please it your majesty
	Command me any service to her thither?
King.	That she vouchsafe me audience for one word.
Boyet.	I will; and so will she, I know, my lord. *[Exit.*
Biron.	This fellow pecks up wit as pigeons peas,
	And utters it again when God doth please:
	He is wit's pedlar, and retails his wares
	At wakes, and wassels, meetings, markets, fairs;
	And we that sell by gross, the Lord doth know,
	Have not the grace to grace it with such show.

This gallant pins the wenches on his sleeve, –
Had he been Adam, he had tempted Eve:
He can carve too, and lisp: why this is he
That, kiss'd away his hand in courtesy;
This is the ape of form, monsieur the nice,
That, when he plays at tables, chides the dice
In honourable terms; nay, he can sing
A mean most meanly; and in ushering,
Mend him who can: the ladies call him sweet;
The stairs, as he treads on them, kiss his feet:
This is the flower that smiles on every one,
To show his teeth as white as whale's bone:
And consciences that will not die in debt
Pay him the due of honey-tongu'd Boyet.

King.   A blister on his sweet tongue, with my heart,
That put Armado's page out of his part!

Biron.   See where it comes! – Behaviour, what wert thou
Till this man show'd thee? and what art thou now?

[*Re-enter the Princess, ushered by Boyet; Rosaline, Maria, Katharine, and Attendants.*

King.   All hail, sweet madam, and fair time of day!

Prin.   Fair, in all hail, is foul, as I conceive.

King.   Construe my speeches better, if you may.

Prin.   Then wish me better, I will give you leave.

King.   We came to visit you; and purpose now
To lead you to our court: vouchsafe it then.

Prin.   This field shall hold me: and so hold your vow:
Nor God, nor I, delight in perjur'd men.

King.   Rebuke me not for that which you provoke;
The virtue of your eye must break my oath.

Prin.   You nickname virtue: vice you should have spoke;
For virtue's office never breaks men's troth.
Now, by my maiden honour, yet as pure
As the unsullied lily; I protest,
A world of torments though I should endure,
I would not yield to be your house's guest:
So much I hate a breaking cause to be

	Of heavenly oaths, vow'd with integrity.
King.	O, you have liv'd in desolation here,
	Unseen, unvisited, much to our shame.
Prin.	Not so, my lord; it is not so, I swear;
	We have had pastime here, and pleasant game;
	A mess of Russians left us but of late.
King.	How, madam! Russians!
Prin.	Ay, in truth, my lord;
	Trim gallants, full of courtship and of state.
Ros.	Madam, speak true. – It is not so, my lord;
	My lady, – to the manner of the days, –
	In courtesy, gives undeserving praise.
	We four, indeed, confronted here with four
	In Russian habit; here they stay'd an hour
	And talk'd apace; and in that hour, my lord,
	They did not bless us with one happy word.
	I dare not call them fools; but this I think,
	When they are thirsty, fools would fain have drink.
Biron.	This jest is dry to me. – Fair, gentle sweet,
	Your wit makes wise things foolish; when we greet
	With eyes best seeing heaven's fiery eye,
	By light we lose light: your capacity
	Is of that nature, that to your huge store
	Wise things seem foolish and rich things but poor.
Ros.	This proves you wise and rich, for in my eye, –
Biron.	I am a fool, and full of poverty.
Ros.	But that you take what doth to you belong,
	It were a fault to snatch words from my tongue.
Biron.	O, I am yours, and all that I possess.
Ros.	All the fool mine?
Biron.	I cannot give you less.
Ros.	Which of the visards was it that you wore?
Biron.	Where? when? what visard? why demand you this?
Ros.	There, then, that visard; that superfluous case
	That hid the worse and show'd the better face.
King.	We are described: they'll mock us now downright.
Dum.	Let us confess, and turn it to a jest.

Prin.	Amaz'd, my lord? why looks your highness sad?
Ros.	Help, hold his brows! he'll swoon! Why look you pale? –
	Sea-sick, I think, coming from Muscovy.
Biron.	Thus pour the stars down plagues for perjury.
	Can any face of brass hold longer out? –
	Here stand I, lady: dart thy skill at me;
	Bruise me with scorn, confound me with a flout;
	Thrust thy sharp wit quite through my ignorance;
	Cut me to pieces with thy keen conceit;
	And I will wish thee never more to dance,
	Nor never more in Russian habit wait.
	O, never will I trust to speeches penn'd,
	Nor to the motion of a school-boy's tongue;
	Nor never come in visard to my friend;
	Nor woo in rhyme, like a blind harper's song:
	Taffeta phrases, silken terms precise,
	Three-pil'd hyperboles, spruce affectation,
	Figures pendantical: these summer-flies
	Have blown me full of maggot ostentation;
	I do forswear them: and I here protest,
	By this white glove, – how white the hand. God knows! –
	Henceforth my wooing mind shall be express'd
	In russet yeas, and honest kersey noes:
	And, to begin, wench, – so God help me, la! –
	My love to thee is sound, sans crack or flaw.
Ros.	Sans sans, I pray you.
Biron.	Yet I have a trick
	Of the old rage: – bear with me, I am sick;
	I'll leave it by degrees. Soft, let us see; –
	Write, Lord have mercy on us, on those three;
	They are infected; in their hearts it lies:
	They have the plague, and caught it of your eyes:
	These lords are visited; you are not free,
	For the Lord's tokens on you do I see.
Prin.	No, they are free that gave these tokens to us.
Biron.	Our states are forfeit: seek not to undo us.
Ros.	It is not so; for how can this be true,

	That you stand forfeit, being those that sue?
Biron.	Peace; for I will not have to do with you.
Ros.	Nor shall not, if I do as I intend.
Biron.	Speak for yourselves; my wit is at an end.
King.	Teach us, sweet madam, for our rude transgression
	Some fair excuse.
Prin.	The fairest is confession.
	Were you not here but even now, disguis'd?
King.	Madam, I was.
Prin.	And were you well advis'd?
King.	I was, fair madam.
Prin.	When you then were here,
	What did you whisper in your lady's ear?
King.	That more than all the world I did respect her.
Prin.	When she shall challenge this you will reject her.
King.	Upon mine honour, no.
Prin.	Peace, peace, forbear;
	Your oath once broke, you force not to forswear.
King.	Despise me when I break this oath of mine.
Prin.	I will; and therefore keep it:– Rosaline,
	What did the Russian whisper in your ear?
Ros.	Madam, he swore that he did hold me dear
	As precious eyesight; and did value me
	Above this world: adding thereto, moreover,
	That he would wed me, or else die my lover.
Prin.	God give thee joy of him! the noble lord
	Most honourably doth uphold his word.
King.	What mean you, madam? by my life, my troth,
	I never swore this lady such an oath.
Ros.	By heaven you did; and, to confirm it plain;
	You gave me this: but take it, sir, again.
King.	My faith and this the princess I did give;
	I knew her by this jewel on her sleeve.
Prin.	Pardon me sir; this jewel she did wear;
	And Lord Biron, I thank him, is my dear:–
	What; will you have me, or your pearl again?
Biron.	Neither of either; I remit both twain.–

I see the trick on't; – here was a consent,
Knowing aforehand of our merriment,
To dash it like a Christmas comedy:
Some carry-tale, some please-man, some slight zany,
Some mumble-news, some trencher-knight, some Dick, –
That smiles his cheek in years, and knows the trick
To make my lady laugh when she's dispos'd, –
Told our intents before: which once disclos'd,
The ladies did change favours; and then we,
Following the signs, woo'd but the sign of she.
Now, to our perjury to add more terror,
We are again forsworn, – in will and error.
Much upon this it is: – and might not you

                                            [*To Boyet.*

Forestal our sport, to make us thus untrue?
Do not you know my lady's foot by the squire,
And laugh upon the apple of her eye?
And stand between her back, sir, and the fire,
Holding a trencher, jesting merrily?
You put our page out: go, you are allow'd;
Die when you will, a smock shall be your shroud.
You leer upon me, do you? there's an eye
Wounds like a leaden sword.

Boyet.   Full merrily
Hath this brave manage, this career, been run.

Biron.   Lo, he is tilting straight! Peace; I have done.

'The Holly Song'

William Shakespeare

Blow, blow, thou Winter Wind,
Thou art not so unkind
As man's ingratitude;

Thy tooth is not so keen,
Because thou art not seen,
Although thy Breath be rude.

Heigh Ho! sing Heigh Ho! unto the Green Holly:
Most Friendship is feigning, most loving mere folly;
Then, heigh ho! the Holly!
This life is most Jolly.

Freeze, freeze, thou bitter Sky,
Thou dost not bite so nigh
As benefits forgot:
Though thou the waters warp,
Thy sting is not so sharp
As Friends remembered not.

Heigh Ho! sing Heigh Ho! unto the Green Holly:
Most Friendship is feigning, most loving mere folly:
Then, heigh ho!, the Holly!
This life is most Jolly.

'Sing heigh ho unto the green holly', from Christmas with the Poets *by the Vitzelly Brothers (1840).*

To Make a Dish of Snow

From A Booke of Cookerie

A recipe for a seasonal-sounding dessert from a late sixteenth-century cookery book entitled A Book of Cookerie *(1594). Such a book may well have been in the possession of Shakespeare's mother, or even of his wife, and the dish would have been familiar to him.*

Take a pottle of sweet thick Cream, and the white of eyght Egs, and beate them altogether, with a spoone, then put them into your cream with a dishfull of Rosewater, and a dishfull of Sugar withall, then take a sticke and make it clene, and then cut it in the end foursquare, and therewith beat all the aforesaid things together, and ever as it ariseth take it off, and put it in to a Cullender, this doone, take a platter and sette an Apple in the midst of it, sticke a thicke bush of Rosemary in the Apple. Then cast your Snow upon the Rosemary and fill your platter therewith, and if you have wafers cast some withall, and so serve them forthe.

Too Good a Bonfire

AN EXTRACT FROM *CHRISTMAS UNDER QUEEN ELIZABETH*

Esme Stuart

Esme Stuart was a student of Elizabethan custom during the Victorian period and believed to be the daughter of Daniel Stuart, an early press baron of note. Her book, the Good old Days *or Christmas under Queen*

Elizabeth tells of the trials of a yeoman farmer and his family in the years of social stability and religious persecution in the latter part of Elizabeth's reign, which sets the scene firmly within the lifespan of Shakespeare. The problems and topical matters in this tale are the same as those which were familiar to the Bard; thus the story helps to paint an accurate picture of life in Shakespeare's England.

In the story, Master Pennyfeather and his family are followers of the English Church established by Henry VIII; they sit between the 'Papists' who followed the old Roman Church and the new 'Puritans' who were establishing themselves. They observed all the old traditions and customs of Christmas, the Yule Log, the house-decorating party, Father Christmas. All these are frowned upon by the children's teacher, Hapgood, who is a Puritan. The heroine, Annys, is in love with Jacob, an English Catholic, and has some puritan leanings, but is betrothed by her father to her cousin, Rowland, who is a courtier, a High Church Royalist and a cold heartless man. The extracts below and elsewhere in this book are concerned with the preparations for Christmas and begin with the bringing in of the Yule log for the Christmas Eve fire and the decorating party – which turns into a rather bigger fire than anticipated:

The master of Sandy's Hollow was in a very bad temper when he entered the yard of his homestead. Things have not gone as they should have done, at least as Master Pennyfeather had intended. The pastor was so much connected with his family that some evil tongues might blazon abroad suspicious facts, and thereby bring him into trouble.

Woe to the unlucky person who first crosses the path of a man in a temper against nobody in particular! To-day the yeoman's wrath burst upon Joe's head as he was lazily wondering whether the Yule Log had best be brought indoors by him, or whether there was the least chance of it bringing itself in.

'Come you vagabond, you lazy dog, bestir yourself! In all my life I never saw such a slow fellow, by my faith!'

Joe too, was in a bad temper from various causes which we need not inquire into, but Joe's temper was in no ways like Master Pennyfeather's. This latter's humour resembled a thundercloud, the former's a volcano. The first eruption was visible when, instead of patiently listening to his master's rebuke as his master meant him to do, he gave an angry kick to the log, as much as to say, 'Would that this were the Master!' The yeoman understood this well enough, and the thunder rolled, then at last broke. We need not put down the string of appellatives which regaled Joe's ears. In the midst Annys put her small hand on her father's shoulder, saying, 'Come, then, dear Father, forgive Joe, and let us quickly re-enter the house; Time presses.' Alas! her Father had already forgotten what Joe's offence was, and so could not forgive it. When he had exhausted his breath he rewarded himself by dismissing Joe from his service.

'There. Rascal, get you gone; I will have no more of such lazy good-for-nothing dogs.' This done, he wiped his forehead and entered the house.

Joe had been quite calmed by his master's last outburst. He took up his jacket which lay on the ground, shook his fist at the empty space which had lately contained Master Pennyfeather, and then muttering, 'Awaw, awaw; he'll soon have a Yule log and bonfire big enough for his big words to burn in!' he turned away and walked off.

'A word with you, if it so please you, good kinsman,' said Rowland Whyte to the yeoman, and at the same time making such a bow that Master Pennyfeather thought with pride on every letter of his name. Aye! it was one to be proud of when the great family of Pennyfeather could reckon amongst its ranks a courtly man who knew how to make such a bow! His brow cleared, and the storm being over, the clouds rolled away.

'Yes, yes, kinsman, one word, and as many as you will; but first let little Annys tell you what has befallen that worthy Hapgood.' Annys did so, and Rowland smiled at her tale, especially when she added imploringly, 'Oh, kind kinsman! I pray you use your influence at Court and get the poor man released. He is so harmless, and moreover, so good!'

'If you get him released, I pray you, Rowland, get him also transported', joined in Eve, who was in a flippant mood. 'I am right sick of being taught by him.'

'I would fain oblige you both, fair coz, but I revere the race of Pennyfeathers too much to care to endanger another head of them. Know you not that one has –'

'Tut, tut! no-one could doubt me! and I trow my head is as firmly fixed on my shoulders as most men's. Ah! Rowland! I see thou hast it not in thy power to help us in this matter; but come with me in private and out with thy matter, now mine is at an end;' and the two men retired.

'I know well what he is going to ask our Father,' said Eve, approaching her sister and looking mysterious, so as to excite her curiosity. 'Why, Annys, how sad thou art! surely the pastor's fate hangs not so heavy on thy mind?'

'He was always kind to me, but I have other matters to sadden me.'

'Annys, what will you give me for telling you a secret?'

'Come, Eve, leave me alone to think, and go seek Ben that he may see after the Yule log. My father has dismissed Joe.'

'Good riddance of bad rubbish, say I; but my secret, Annys; well, I must tell thee: Rowland Whyte is such a fair spoken gentleman! He has been saying a hundred pretty things to me while you were out; among others he said, "And would you not take me for a brother, Mistress Eve?" That was all because I said I would have naught to do with a courtier. I could lay a wager he is now asking thy hand from our Father.'

'Eve, how canst thou talk so!'

'Aye, but I do;' and hardly had she spoken the words when Master Pennyfeather and Rowland entered the room with smiling faces. Her father noticed Annys's scarlet cheeks.

'Eh, eh! what little bird has been whispering? Come, my Annys, spare thy blushes a little; thou must e'en look up and listen to the fair proposals that Rowland is about –'

'Nay, nay, father! Indeed I am –' began poor Annys in her confusion, making no sense of her words, which allowed Rowland to believe he was coyly accepted; and before anything else could be said there were shouts of – 'Here it comes, make way – make way for our bonny Yule log!' All but Annys and her father rushed out to give a helping hand with the Yule log over the threshold, as it was thought unlucky not to have laid at least one finger on the wood as it passed through the door sill.

'Annys' said the yeoman, sternly for him, 'what means this scene? If it be Jacob thou art hankering after, I tell thee plainly, thou wilt never be his wife, and so thou hadst better set thy face towards Rowland. Such a gallant, such a comely young man, and so fair-spoken: he has just told me he will take thee to court, and that the queen will raise thee high. Eve may yet, through thee, marry a rich nobleman, who knows?' Then seeing Annys still weeping, 'I command thee wench to have done with these fooleries, and give some word of welcome to thy future husband, or by my troth – but here he comes. Good Rowland, Annys will follow out my wishes, and thou must forgive her if surprise and – but young people understand each other;' and so saying, the master, glad to have got over the part of an angry father, was happy enough to laugh over the Yule log.

Feeding the poor in the seventeenth century, from 'A Christmas Carroll' (illustration by Frank Merrill, 1895).

Annys was much too shy to utter a word in answer to strings of courtly phrases, which indeed she scarcely heard, and when the hall became full with people, and she was free to retire, she went to her chamber and cried her heart out.

'Hurrah for Christmas-tide!' Everyone ought to be happy, thought Annys, but she was not; to her it was 'Woe to Christmas Eve'. At this minute Dame Pennyfeather hurried into the room not being aware of what had happened.

'Come, Annys, haste ye below stairs, for such a company has come in! The maids and myself can scarce serve all the folk. The song is just about to tune up: thou hast missed the placing of the log.' The girl dared not disobey, and before she could reach the hall, music or noise of all descriptions began, and then burst forth the song of the Yule log:

> Come, bring with a noise,
> My merry, merry boys,
> The Christmas log to the firing,
> While my good Dame, she
> Bids ye all be free,
> And drink to your heart's desiring.

Light the new block, and
For good success in his spending,
On your psalteries play,
That sweet luck may
Come, while the log is a teending.

Drink now the strong beer,
Cut the white loaf here
The while the meat is a shredding,
For the rare minc'd pie
And the plums stand by
To fill the paste that's a-kneading

'This is blythesome, sweet Mistress Annys', whispered Rowland in her ear, 'and I wager that "sweet luck" will soon be ours.'

'I love not such sport', returned she shortly, 'and see, sir, your help is wanted to decorate the rafters; I pray you, lend a hand.'

Thus dismissed, Rowland went among the crowd, and before the evening was over had said some pretty speeches to all the girls in the room, and had drunk as freely as if he were not a courtier. Annys thought bitterly that he did not behave as one heart-smitten. Jacob would not have done the same. Annys could not guess what the night would bring forth, or she would not have bemoaned herself so much, I fancy.

It was twelve o'clock at night. Sandy's Hollow was at last quiet, the Yule log had burnt down quite low, the dogs lay sleeping on the mats, here and there a cat walked softly about, and Christmas Eve was dead. One of the inhabitants of the house was, however, tossing restlessly on her soft bed, and this person was no other than Eve. I very much fear that her supper had disagreed with her, for in spite of everything she could do, sleep would not come. Annys had fallen asleep in the act of shedding tears, but as Eve did not know this, she began envying her sister's quiet repose. Presently thinking that if she went to look out of the window she might become suddenly sleepy, she softly got out of bed, walked across the room on tip-toe, and drew away the heavy curtain. The night was very dark, but the snow lighted up the ground. Eve was just about to go back to bed, seeing nothing to amuse her, when she suddenly perceived a dark object against the snow, and the light of a lantern. Presently the light was put out and the figure disappeared around the corner. Eve, whose courage was not of any high order, made but one leap back into bed, and had soon hidden her head under the clothes. In spite of this, sleep came not, and for an hour more she lay bemoaning her fate and inventing a pathetic tale for the next day. Her waking thoughts at last became confused and she dreamt that it was Midsummer Eve instead of Christmas Eve. It was quite warm; the sun was shining, and Ben was just going to light the bonfire.

'Oh! Ben, wait there till I can get out of the smoke', she said in her dream; but this woke her. She started up in bed to find the room was indeed full of smoke. I am sorry to say she entirely forgot her sister, but in one instant she had opened her door and stepped into the passage. The room the sisters occupied was, as I have mentioned, at one end of a wing of the old house, and quite distant from the centre of the dwelling. What was Eve's horror to find the passage so filled with smoke that she could not breathe! The end of the wing must be on fire! Her door banged to, and she flew though the smoke, taking but two seconds to reach her mother's room.

'Mother! father! the house is on fire!' But the discovery had already been made by the servants, who, in all sorts of costumes, came rushing towards Master Pennyfeather's chamber. Amelia was there, wringing her hands and saying she knew she was on fire, and of course would be burnt.

'Hold thy tongue, Amelia!' cried Eve; 'why think only of thyself: are we not all in danger? Fetch me a kirtle and shawl.'

I need not describe the scene of bustle which ensued; the panic was so great that all the household turned out of doors except the yeoman. His wife had found some difficulty in waking him, but once out of bed he was all activity. Setting everyone to work with authority, he cried – 'It is only the wing, my men, that is on fire! Don't let it be said that the fire conquered a Pennyfeather! There now! let the women keep out of the way, and let us get as much water as possible!'

The snow was melting round the burning wing, and made the footing dangerous. It was a glorious scene however, and Rowland Whyte, who had been far removed from the part on fire, had therefore had time to dress himself quite elegantly, said calmly, 'It is worth seeing Dame Pennyfeather; I would not have missed the sight for twenty marks!'

At this minute Eve rushed up almost beside herself with grief. 'Oh, mother, mother! Annys! It is all my fault; I forgot her: I pray you, Rowland, save her! See! See! Up there at that first story! The fire has not yet reached her, but the smoke! Oh, Help! Help!'

The yeoman heard these words and turned pale. 'Annys, Annys! How is this? What! Still in her room? Cowards! Thieves! Rascals! Why did you not tell me? Here, James, Bracy, your weight in gold if you can get the ladders. I forgot; here is Rowland Whyte. Ah, my boy! I know thy heart has leapt up there already though – but come, haste, there is the door Rowland; that way may still be safe. What man! Why tarry?'

'I would indeed risk everything', said Rowland, edging back, 'but good sir, this is an impossibility. Eve had best shout to her to throw herself from the window.'

The men were now bringing the ladders, but the confusion was great. The yeoman, however, found time to say, 'Thou craven! Thinkest thou that such as thou shalt have her? I would rather the flames devour her. Art not thou ashamed to be standing there in lace ruff, to boot?' and so saying, the despairing father rushed toward the ladder himself, when a hand, firm and strong, put him aside.

'This is my business, good Master Pennyfeather; you cannot endanger your life: but if I die it will be for her.'

It was Jacob Buckstone, who having seen the fire had run all the way from his farm and had been greeted with the news that Annys had not been able to escape, for that the passage in the wing was impassable. It was no easy matter to ascend the ladder, for the gable was tottering already, the fire below having eaten away at some of its supports; moreover, no Annys appeared at the window, which was closed. Jacob almost feared that she had suffocated before she was aware of her danger. Carefully and steadily he mounted, knowing that more haste often makes less speed, and that Annys's only chance might thus be lost. He had no time to feel anxiety: his whole mind was concentrated on the job in hand.

At last his head was level with the sill of the window, and raising his voice he cried, 'Annys! Annys! Haste, I beseech thee!' Nothing answered him, and with one blow he burst through the glass and looked in. A sudden gust of wind happily cleared the room for one instant, of the smoke, but what availed this? Jacob, with one glance could see no-one, only a heap of clothes in one corner, which Jacob in the agony of the moment, fancied must be Annys lying dead. It only needed this sight to make him desperate. With one bound he entered the room and felt his way to the corner. The heap of blankets contained no living person. But where could she be? Even the brave Jacob dared not open the door of the room, knowing the draught would end all hope of escape. He now heard voices shouting something from below. . . . His head dazed, he made a few steps towards the window. . . . More shouts from below, a great cloud of smoke rolling slowly up, then a voice distinctly heard above the rest woke Jacob from his torpor. It was Annys's accent, and he seized the ladder and shook it; still the maiden called, 'Oh, Jacob, Jacob! make haste; I am safe, quite safe, oh Jacob!. . .' The flames only a few feet away from him began to throw out their long thin, cruel arms, as if eager to clutch their prey, but at every second they hid themselves away as a bucket of water was thrown at them. Then how spitefully they hissed, angry at the disturbance to their plan; again they darted forward despite their foes. . . . Hurrah! they had almost touched the giant who is descending the frail ladder . . .

There was a cry of despair from Annys, then Jacob fell heavily to the ground. Happily the height was not great, and gentle hands came at once to his help. Annys, who would not be restrained, pushed her way through the crowd and knelt down on the earth to gaze at his face. The silly one took his motionless and closed eyes as signs that death had taken him from her, and cried out,

'Oh, Jacob, Jacob! Would that I had died instead of thee, alack!'

A groan was her answer, but never was groan more welcome; the girl's spirits rose immediately, and seeing Maurice, she said, 'Brother, dear, help me carry him into the barn, away from this bustle. Ah! I forgot; thy poor arm is hurt: why am I to be the cause of so much pain?' Two men were however, ordered by Master Pennyfeather to do her bidding, and very soon ministering to the sick man gave Annys plenty of occupation. The rest of the women followed their example and retired to the barn, while the men renewed their efforts toward putting out the fire. Master Pennyfeather, relieved from anxiety, worked like a very Hercules, and before five o'clock struck from the hall clock there was a shout of, 'Three cheers for Sandy's Hollow and good Master Pennyfeather!'

The worthy man doffed his fur cap and said reverently, 'All praise to God, my men, that He has left some portion standing; aye, enough to shelter us and any poor folk who may pass by this night. Now look you carefully round, boys, so as not to tread on any burning brand.' So saying, he left the farm men to get the rubbish somewhat in order, and went to the barn to see with his own eyes that all were safe and sound this Christmas night.

'The Christmas Feast'

Eric Bennett

This is a short discourse on the festive board of the early sixteenth century, by the food writer for the Tatler *in the 1950s, Eric Bennett. This delicious list of festive foods had evolved from much less palatable fare from the previous century, and was, alas, only to enjoy a short period of success before the Commonwealth arrived with its ensuing problems.*

It was little more than two years before the end of Elizabeth I's reign. The Armada had been defeated, and England was established as a great Power. It was the year Shakespeare wrote *As You Like It*. The year before Spenser died, and Ben Jonson had written *Every Man Out Of His Humour*. It was the climax of a Golden Age in our history. But can one wonder that they wrote so nobly and fought so boldly when they ate so well?

1600. During the sixteenth century the Turkey had been introduced to England, but the Goose was still the favourite bird and the most popular Christmas Dish was Roast Beef.

The Christmas Dinner was still confined to three courses, but the courses had grown more elaborate. The first course might run to thirty-two dishes. Sixteen of them were 'full dishes' (NB, proper recipes as opposed to what we now call 'nibbles').

Shield of Brawn with Mustard, boiled capon, boiled beef, roast beef, roast pork, roasted neats tongues (NB, ox tongue), baked chewets – these were pies containing finely chopped meats with spices – roast goose, roast swan, roast turkey, roast haunch of venison, venison pasty, a kid with pudding in belly, olive pie, roast capons, and a custard. The other sixteen

The Christmas procession, from an 1860 Christmas card.

were salads, fricassees and pastries of various kinds.

Fish and Game came with the second course with a choice from cod's head, salmon, smelts, shrimps, lobsters, prawns, sturgeon, woodcock, snipes, smews, and lark pie.

The sweets had become more recognizably Christmassy. In addition to fruit jellies and syllabubs, there were minc'd pies, Christmas pie, and plum porridge.

Plum porridge was a plum pudding cooked without a cloth and served in a tureen. Christmas Pie was a formidable dish, according to one recipe, ' it is a most learned mixture of neats tongues, chicken, eggs, sugar, raising, lemon and orange peel, and various kinds of spicery'.

Strong ale was still a favourite drink. It was no longer all home brewed; there were twenty-six breweries in London alone. The hot spiced ale of the Wassail Bowl was still popular, though now it was known as 'Lambs Wool'.

Home-made cherry brandy and cordials were preferred to wine, but sack-posset, made from hot milk curdled with Canary wine, or sherry was the stuff to get the party going – as Falstaff well knew!

'A Tale of a Merrie Christmas Caroll'

From Pasquil's Jests

This story of carol singers, found in Pasqil's Jests *and published in 1609, shows the humour of the time and might even have been told in Christmas company during Shakespeare's seasons in London. As the*

former Queen Elizabeth I had placed such importance on the lords going home to their estates for Christmas with their tenants, maybe this story was an endorsement of her wishes. This tale has, in Victorian times, been linked to a poetic legend about the Squire of Gamwell Hall in the twelfth century. Whether the poet used the tale recorded in Pasquil, or whether Pasquil used a much older tale to tell I have not been able to find out.

There was sometime an old knight, who being disposed to make himself merry in a Christmas time, sent for many of his tenants and poore neighbours, with their wives, to dinner; when, having made meat to be set on the table, would suffer no man to drinke, till he that was master ouer his wife should sing a carroll, to excuse all the company. Greate nicenesse there was, who should bee the musician, now the cuckow time was so farre off. Yet, with much adoe, looking one upon another, after a dry hemme or two,

The Christmas pie, from 'A Christmas Carroll' (illustration by Frank Merrill, 1895).

a dreaming companion drew out as much as hee durst, towards an ill-fashioned ditty.

When having made an end, to the great comfort of the beholders, at last it came to the women's table, where, likewise, commandment was given, that there should no drinke bee touched till she that was master ouer her husband had sung a Christmas carroll; whereupon they fell all to such a singing, that there was never heard such a catterwalling peece of musicke; whereat the knight laughed heartily that it did him half as much good as a corner of his Christmas pie!

'Now Thrice Welcome Christmas!'

George Wither

Now thrice welcome Christmas,
Which brings us good cheer,
Minc'd pies and Plum Porridge,
Good Ale and strong Beer;
With Pig, Goose & Capon,
The best that can be;
So well doth the weather
And our Stomachs agree.

Observe how the Chimneys
Do smoke all about,
The cooks are providing
For dinner, no doubt;
But those on whose tables
No Victuals appear,
O, may they keep Lent
For the rest of the Year!

Decking the house with evergreens, from W. Sandys' Christmastide *(1830).*

With Holly and Ivy
So green and so gay,
We deck up our Houses
As fresh as the Day.
With Bays and Rosemary,
And Laurel complete;
And everyone now is a King in conceit.

'Of Scented Smoaks and Washballs'

AN ELIZABETHAN RECIPE

*In Shakespeare's time there were no chemists with vast arrays
of perfumes, soaps and room fresheners or simple remedies to buy at
will. Elizabethan housewives, such as Mary Arden, Shakespeare's
mother, and Anne, his wife, had to make their own, and their
personal receipt books would have had a number of recipes for such
things, usually placed at the opposite end of the book to the
culinary recipes. Such recipes are very fashionable in the
second Elizabethan era and, with one or two ingredients not now
available omitted, could be used equally well today. The following
are taken from the manuscript of an early seventeenth-century
receipt book.*

A Perfume to Smoak and burn:

Take Labdanum two ounces, Storax one ounce, Cloves and Mace of each
half an ounce. Ten grains each of Musk and Civet [Alternatives to these can
be had from such shops as Body Shop]. Grind all in a mortar with a stone
pestle until fine pouder. Then add to this pouder Mucilage of Gum
Tragacanth and water and make into small cakes, and let to dry. These you
can then put amongst your linens and cloathes to scent. Also when occasion
requires, put into a chafing dish with coals and let the smoak perfume the
air.

For the good washball:

Of Venetian Soap take six ounces, cloves two ounces, Labdanum, Aniseeds
of each one ounce; then of Nutmegs, Marjorum, Cypress powder,
Geranium Moschatum, Camphire of each half an ounce. Storax liquida
half a drachm, Musk ten grains, all being into a fine pouder and with a

little fine sugar beat all in a mortar then shape into WASHBALLS and dry same and put away for use. If you put them into your linens, they will scent these until needed.

The following is a recipe which was used on the faces of the young men who needed smooth complexions for their female roles in theatrical companies.

To take away Hair:

Take the shells of fifty-two eggs and still them with a good fire, and with the water anoint yourself where you would have the hair off: Or else Cat's dung, that is hard and dryed, beaten to a powder, and tempered with strong vinegar, and anointed on the place.

To counteract the red faces caused by bilious digestion and too much drink there were a number of suitable recipes. The following might well have been among the useful receipts in the 'household' book of the players.

An Excellent oyl to take away the heat and shining of the Nose:

Take 12 ounce of Gourd Feed, crackle them, take out the kernels, peel off the skin, and blanch six ounces of bitter Almonds, and make an Oyl of them, and anoint the place grieved therewith. You must always take as much of the Gourd feed as Almonds. Use it often.

And for pimples:

Take the Liverwort that groweth in the Well, stamp it and strain it, and put the juyce into cream, and so anoint your face. Proven.

Please note that the author has not tried all of these recipes, and cannot guarantee their efficacy. It should be remembered that they are taken from original seventeenth-century sources and are fun to try as a novelty rather than as prescribed remedies!

Shakespeare's 'Popish Kingdom'

From a translation of the German by
Barnaby Googe

Despite its title, the following account in blank verse by Barnaby Googe,
1570, gives an excellent picture of the customs associated with
Christmas in Elizabethan England, especially those traditionally
observed by the young. Here are described carolling, looking for a
husband, divining his characteristics; a rather muddled idea of the
observances of the Christmas Mass and Church customs of Christmas
Eve and Day; then the custom of blood letting of horses on St Stephen's
Day (26 December), St John's Day when it was believed that to eat
blessed wine and cake would grant them health during the coming year,
and Holy Innocents which was traditionally a day of fasting,
chastisement and penitence. This was followed by New Year with its
gifts and parties which began on this day and continued through to
Twelfth Night. There were customs common to every household:
Twelfth Eve King, the university customs of the Christmas Prince, the
Twelfth Night cake with its token which when found makes the finder
king for the evening and the house blessings and the blessing of the
Senses to keep them good and pure – which in earlier times when village
communities were smaller, would have been done by the parish priest,
but by Shakespeare's day were done by the master of the household. All
are disreputed, yet preserved for posterity in Googe's verse.
Shakespeare was born into a time of religious upheaval. His father
was a known recusant, a follower of the old Roman Catholic faith
banned by Henry VIII. It is thought that his mother, Mary Arden, was
also a recusant, which would explain how a tenant could ask for his
Lord's daughter's hand in marriage. The ancient and wealthy Catholic
Ardens preferred to have a lowly son-in-law of the same faith than any
other in those troubled times. For a while under Queen Mary, and

during the early days of Elizabeth's reign, they would have been able to practise their faith openly, but their children would have had to be brought up in the established Church, at least officially. Most recusant families brought their children up in the old faith in secret, so it is probable that William was at least nominally a follower of the old faith in his youth. Therefore, the writing of those such as Barnaby Googe would have been both an annoyance and an amusement to him. In his fanaticism, Googe little realized that he was guilty of keeping alive the memory of Christmas customs which otherwise might have died out completely.

As a man, Shakespeare himself, as far as we know, followed the English Church established by King Henry, which for many people did not seem to be so far removed from the old religion. There was, already, evidence of Puritan development, which was coming across to Britain from North-Western Europe. One advocate of this tide of puritanical teaching was Thomas Kirchmaier, a German writer in 1553, whose book, Regnum Papisticum *was translated as* The Popish Kingdom *by Barnaby Googe in 1570. Below is his description of Christmas under Queen Elizabeth I and if one looks beyond the sourness of the description there are several references to traditional customs of the time, and one or two which the young Will might have participated in around his neighbours' houses in Stratford-upon-Avon.*

Three weeks before the day whereon was born the Lord of grace,
And on the Thursday boys and girls do run in every place,
And bounce and beat at every door, with blows and lusty snaps
And cry, the advent of the Lord, not born as yet, perhaps:
And wishing to the neighbours all, that in the houses dwell,
A happy year and everything to spring and prosper well:
Here have they pears and plums, and pence, each man gives willingly,
For these three nights are always thought unfortunate to be:
Wherein they are afraid of sprites and cankered witche's spite,
And dreadful devils, black and grim, that then have chiefest might.

In these same days young wanton girls that meet for marriage be,
Do search to know the names of them, that shall their husbands be.
Four onions, five or eight they take, and make in every one

Presenting the Wassail Bowl in Elizabethan times, from Christmas with the Poets *by the Vitzelly Brothers (1840).*

Such names as they do fancy most, and best do think upon.
Thus near the chimney then they set, and that same onion than
The first doth sprout doth surely bear the name of their good man.
Their husband's nature eke they seek to know, and all his guise;
When as the sun hath hid himself, and left the starry skies,
Unto some woodstack do they go, and while they there do stand,

Each one draws out a faggot stick, the next that comes to hand,
Which if straight and even be, and have no knots at all,
A gentle husband then they think shall surely to them fall.
But if it foul and crooked be, and knotty here and there,
A crabbed churlish husband then they earnestly do fear.

These things the wicked Papists bear, and suffer willingly,
Because they neither do the end, nor fruits of faith espie:
And rather had the people should obey their foolish lust,
Than truly God to know, and in him here alone to trust.
Then comes the day wherein the Lord did bring his birth to pass,
Whereas at midnight up they rise, and every man to mass.
This time so holy counted is, that divers earnestly
Do think the waters all to wine are changed suddenly:
In that same hour that Christ himself was born, and came to light
And unto water straight again transformed and altered quite.

There are beside that mindfully the money still do watch,
The first to altar comes, which then they privily do snatch.
The priests lest other should it have takes oft the same away,
Whereby they think throughout the year to have good luck in play,
And not to lose: then straight at game till daylight do they strive,
To make some present proof how well their hallowed pence will thrive.
Three masses every priest doth sing upon that solemn day,
With offerings unto everyone, that so the more may play.

This done, a wooden child in clouts is on the altar set,
About the which both boys and girls do dance, and trimly jet,
And carols sing in praise of Christ, and for to help them here,
The organ answers every verse, with sweet and solemn cheer.
The priests do roar aloud, and round about the parents stand,
To see the sport, and with their voice do help them and their hand.
Thus wont the Coribants perhaps upon the mountain Ide,
The crying noise of Jupiter new born with song to hide,
To dance about him round, and on their brazen pans to beat,
Lest that his father finding him, should him destroy and eat.

Then following Saint Stephen's Day, whereon doth every man
His horses jaunt and course abroad, as swiftly as he can.
Until they do extremely sweat, and then they let them blood,
For this being done upon this day, they say doth do them good,
And keep them from all maladies and sickness through the year,
As if that Stephen any time took charge of horses here.

Next John the son of Zebedee hath his appointed day,
Who once by cruel tyrants will constrained was, they say,
Strong poison up to drink, and therefore the Papists do believe,
That whoso puts their trust in him, no poison can them grieve.
The wine beside that hallowed is, in worship of his name,
The priests do give the people that bring money for the same.
And after with the selfsame wine are little manchets made,
Against the boistrous winter storms, and sundry suchlike trade;
The men upon this solemn day do take this holy wine,
To make them strong, so do the maids, to make them fair and fine.

Then comes the day that calls to mind the cruel Herod's strife,
Who, seeking Christ to kill, the King of everlasting life,
Destroyed the infants young, a beast unmerciless,
And put to death all such as were of two years old or less.
To them the sinful wretches cry, and earnestly do pray,
To get them pardon for their faults, and wipe their sins away.
The parents when this day appears, do beat their children all
(Though nothing they deserve), and servants all to beating fall.
And monks do whip each other well, or else their prior great,
Or Abbot mad, doth take in hand their breeches all to beat.
In worship of these innocents, or rather as we see,
In honour of the cursed king who did this cruelty.

The next to this is New Year's Day, whereon to every friend
They costly presents in do bring and New Year's gifts do send.
These gifts the husband gives his wife and father eke the child,
And master on his men bestows the like, with favours mild,
And good beginning of the year they wish and wish again,
According to the ancient guise of heathen people vain,

These eight days no man doth require his debts of any man,
Their tables they do furnish out with all the meat they can:
With marchpanes, tarts, and custards great they drink with staring eyes,
They rout and revel, feed and feast, as merry as the pies,
As if they should at the entrance of this New Year have to die,
Yet would they have their bellies full and ancient friends ally.

The wise men's day here followeth, who out from Persia far,
Brought gifts and presents unto Christ, conducted by a star.
The Papists do believe that these were kings, and so them call,
And do affirm that of the same there were but three in all.

Adoration of the Magi, from W. Sandys' Christmastide *(1830).*

Here sundry friends together come, and meet in company,
And make a king amongst themselves by voice or destiny;
Who after princely guise appoints his officers alway,
Then unto feasting do they go, and long time after play:
Upon their Boards in order thick the dainty dishes stand,
Till that their purses empty be and creditors at hand.
Their children herein follow them, and choosing princes here
With pomp and great solemnity they meet and make good cheer
With money either got by stealth, or of their parents eft,
That so they may be trained to know both riot here and theft.

Then every householder to his ability,
Doth make a mighty cake, that may suffice his company:
Herein a penny doth he put, before it comes to fire,
This he divides according to his household doth require;
And every piece distributeth, as round about they stand
Which in their names unto the poor is given out of hand;
But whoso chanceth on the piece wherein the money lies
Is counted king amongst them all, and is with shouts and cries
Exhalted to the heavens up, who taking chalk in hand,
Doth make a cross on every beam and rafters as they stand:
Great force and power have these against all injuries and harms
Of cursed devils, sprites and bugs, of conjuring and charms.
So much this king can do, so much the crosses bring to pass,
Made by some servant, maid or child, or by some foolish ass.

Twice six nights then from Christmas do they count with diligence,
Wherein each master in his house doth burn up frankincense :
And on the table sets a loaf, when night approacheth near,
Before the coals, and frankincense be perfumed there:
First bowing down his head he stands, and nose and ears and eyes,
He smokes, and with his mouth receives the fume that doth arise:
Whom followeth straight his wife, and doth the same full solemnly,
And of their children every one, and all their family:
Which doth preserve, they say, their teeth, and nose and eyes and ear,
From every kind of malady, and sickness all the year.
When every one received hath this odour great and small,

Then one takes up the pan with coals, and frankincense and all
Another takes the loaf, whom all the rest do follow here,
And round the house they go, with torch or taper clear,
That neither meat do want, nor witch with dreadful charm
Have power to hurt their children, or to do their cattle harm.

There are that three nights only to perform this foolish gear,
To this intent, and think themselves safe all year.
To Christ dare none commit himself. And in these days beside
They judge what weather all the year shall happen and betide:
Ascribing to each day a month, and at this present time
The youth in every place do flock, and all appareled fine,
With pipers through the streets they run, and sing at every door
In commendation of the man rewarded well therefore,
Which on themselves they do bestow, or on the church as tho'
The people were not plagued with rogues and begging friars enow.

There cities are where boys and girls together still do run,
About the street with like, as soon as night begins to come,
And bring abroad their wassail bowls, who well rewarded be
With cakes and cheese and great good cheer and money plenteously.

Wassailing the apple trees. A photogravure by Wright & Stokes (1910).

'O Sweetest Night'

Myles Pinkney

Myles Pinkney was a recusant priest, 1599–1674, who wrote several short religious poems redolent of the pre-Reformation era, one of which is reproduced here.

O sweetest Night! My mind I ne'er can wean
From thoughts of Thee, in which the heavens do rain
Huge showers of Grace: the hillocks flow with sweets,
And from the mountains milk and honey sweats.
O sweetest Night! my starved soul doth die
To have a full draught of thy ambrosy.
Tertullian gravely said: 'Some goods there are
As well as evils, which e'en oppress and bear
Us to the ground'. The wonders of this Night
Are such, to find our God in such a plight:
That hardly such a bastard soul is found
Who sends no knees and hearty to kiss the ground.

The Order of Christmas

AN ACCOUNT OF CHRISTMAS AT THE COURT OF ELIZABETH

From Dugdale's Origines Juridiciales

Extracts from Sir William Dugdale's Origines Juridiciales *(1666) of the daily arrangements and the duties of the various officers and servants during the twelve days of Christmas at the Court of Queen Elizabeth*

*some eighty to one hundred years earlier are reproduced here. Copies
(near complete) in English are reproduced in a number of works,
including the Christmas reference works of Dawson (1903) and John
Ashton (1893).*

First it hath been the duty of the Steward to produce five fat Brawns, Vessels, Wood, and other necessities belonging to the kitchen; as also all manner of Spices, Flesh, Fowl, and other Cates for the kitchin.

The office of the chief Butler to provide a rich cupboard of Plate, Silver and Parcel-gilt; seaven dozen of Silver and Parcel-gilt spoons; twelve fair Saltcellars, likewise Silver and Gilt; Twenty Candlesticks of the like.

Twelve fine large Tablecloths of Damask and Diaper, Twenty dozen of Napkins suitable at the least. Three dozen of fair large Towells; whereof the Gentlemen Sewers and Butlers of the house, to have every of them one at mealtimes, during their attendance. Likewise to provide carving knives; twenty dozen of white Cups and green Potts; a Carving Table; Torches; Bread; Beer, and Ale. And the chief of the Butlers was to give attendance on the highest Table in the Hall, with Wine, Ale, and Beer; and all the other Butlers to attend at the other tables in like sort.

The Cupboard of Plate is to remain in the Hall on Christmas Day, St. Stephan's Day and New Yeare's Day. Upon the Banquetting night it was removed to the Butry; which in all respects was very laudably performed.

The office of the Constable Marshall to provide for his employment, a fair gilt compleat Harneys, with a nest of Fethers in the Helm; a fair Poleaxe to bear in his hand, to be chevalrously ordered on Christmas Day and other days, as afterwards is shewed; touching the ordering and settling of all which ceremonies, during the said Grand Christmas, a solemn consultation was held at their Parliament* in the House; in the form following:

First, at the Parliament kept in their Parliament Chamber in this House, on the Even at Night of St. Thomas the Apostle, Officers are to attend, according as they have been long before that time, at a former Parliament, named and elected to undergo several offices for this time of solemnity, honour, and pleasance; of which officers these are the most emminent; namely, the Steward, Marshall, Constable Marshall, Butler, and Master of the Game.

---

* The Parliament being not the government as we know it, but a specially elected group to preside over the Christmas proceedings and orderings.

These Officers are made known and elected in Trinity Term next before; and to have knowledge thereof by letters, in the country, to the end they may prepare themselves against All-Hallow-tide; that, if such nominated officers happen to fail, others may then be chosen in their rooms. The other Officers are appointed at other times nearer Christmas Day.

Christmas Eve. – The Marshall at dinner is to place at the highest Table's end, and next to the Library, all on one side thereof, and most antient persons in the company present: the Dean of the Chappel next to him; then an antient of Bencher, beneath him. At the other end of the table, the Sewer, Cupbearer, and Carver. At the upper end of the Bench-table, the King's Searjeant and Chief Butler; and when the Steward hath served in, and set on the table the first mess, then he is also to sit down.

The order of seating continues with the Master of Revels, the Ranger, Master of Game, etc. down to the Clerk of the Souse tub even! Then begins the ritual of table dressing with the silver plate, linens and salts, trenchers and bread, all in the correct order of laying. A modern student of 'silver service' does not know how easy the order of service is now compared with that of Shakespeare's time.

At the first course the Minstrells must sound their instruments, and go before; and the Steward and Marshall are next to follow together; and after them the Gentleman Sewer; and then cometh the meat. Those three officers are to make together three solemn courtesies, at three several times, between the Skreen and the upper Table; and the second at the midst; and the third at the other end; and then standing by the Sewer performeth his Office.

Whilst the tables are set according to strict ritual, there was: Musick must stand at the Harth side, with the noise of their Musick, their faces direct towards the highest Table; and that done, to return to the Butry with their Musick sounding.

This ritual followed for the second course also, the music now becoming more pervasive after the eating, with songs as well as music.

Then after a little repose, the persons at the highest table arise and prepare to revells: in which time, the Butlers, and other Servitors with them, are to dine in the Library. At both the doors of the Hall are Porters to view the comers in and out at Meal times; to each of them is allowed a cast of Bread and a Caudle nightly after Supper.

At Night before Supper there are Revells and Dancing, and so also after Supper during the twelve daies of Christmass; the antientest Master of the Revells is, after Dinner and Supper, to sing a Caroll or Song; and command other Gentlemen then there present to sing with him and the Company, and so it is very decently performed.

A repast at Dinner is eight pence.

Christmass Day – Service in the Church ended, the Gentlemen presently repair into the Hall to Breakfast, with Brawn, Mustard and Malmsey.

The description of laying the tables for dinner continues in much the same vein as before.

At the first course, is served a fair and large Bore's-head upon a Silver Platter, with Minstralsye. Two Gentlemen in Gowns are to attend at Supper,

The constable marshal and his officers escort the boar's head into the court of Queen Elizabeth I, from W. Sandys' Christmastide *(1830).*

and to bear two fair Torches of Wax next before the Musicians and Trumpetters, and to stand above the Fire with the Musick till the first Course be served in through the Hall. Which performed they, with the Musick, are to return to the Butry. The like course is to be observed in all things, during the time of Christmass. The like at Supper.

A repast at Dinner is twelve shillings.

Then there follows another religious service after dinner. Christmas Day being more solemn than the days which follow.

St. Stephen's Day – This day the Steward, Carver and Cup-Bearer are to serve as afore. After the first course served in, the Constable-Marshall cometh into the Hall, arrayed with fair rich compleat Harneys, white and bright, and gilt, with a nest of Fethers of all colours upon his Crest or Helm, and a gilt Poleaxe in his hand: to whom is associate the Lieutenant of the Tower, armed with a fair white Armour, a nest of Fethers in his Helm, and a like Poleaxe in his hand; and with them sixteen trumpetters; four Drums and Fifes going in rank before them; and with them attendeth four men in white Harneys, from the middle upwards, and Halberds in their hands, bearing on their shoulders the Tower: which persons with the Drums, Trumpetts and Musick, go three times about the Fire. Then the Constable-Marshall, after two or three curtesies made, kneeleth down before the Lord Chancellor; behind him the Lieutenant; and they kneeling, the Constable Marshall pronounceth an oration of a quarter of an hour's length, thereby declaring the purpose of his coming; and that his purpose is to be admitted into his Lordship's service.

Then cometh the Master of the Game, apparelled in green Velvet, and the Ranger of the Forest also, in a green Suit of Satten; bearing in his hand a green Bow and divers Arrows, with wither of them a Hunting Horn about their necks; blowing together three blasts of venery, they pace around the Fire three times. Then the Master of the Game maketh three courtesies, as aforesaid.

Then proceedeth the second course.

At Supper the Hall is to be served with all solemnity, as upon Christmasday. Supper ended, the Constable-Marshall presenteth hisself with Drums afore him, mounted upon a Scaffold, born by four Men, and goeth three times about the Harth, crying out loud, 'A Lord, A Lord' etc. then he decendeth and goeth to dance etc., and after he calleth his Court every one by name, one by one in this manner:

Sir Francis Flatterer of Fowlshurst in the County of Buckingham.

Sir Randle Rakabite, of Rascall-hall, in the County of Rakehell.

Sir Morgan Mumchance, of Much Monkery, in the County of Mad Mopery.

Sir Bartholomew Balbreech, of Buttocksbury, in the County of Brekenock.

This done the Lord of Misrule addresses himself to the Banquet: which ended with some Minstralsye, Mirth and Dancing, every Man departeth to rest.

Every repast is six pence.

Here it should be explained to those not initiated into the mysteries of the Christmas Revels that the ceremony described above is the beginning of the fun and games part of Christmas, the religious observances over for the time being. The Constable Marshal has announced who his Revels Court will be and given them the outlandish names, by which characters he wishes them to behave. This 'Court' will preside over all the revels now until Twelfth Night.

To Make Buttered Oranges

A CHRISTMAS DESSERT RECIPE

Oranges were an expensive fruit and the following sixteenth/early seventeenth-century recipe might have been a special Christmas dessert.

Take a pint of Creame, raspe the peels of two Oranges into half a pint of water or Orange juice, six eggs, two whites, as much suger as will sweeten it, straine and set over a fire. When it is thick put a piece of Butter as big as a Egg and keep it stirring till cold.

'December' Sonnet

William Shakespeare

In his sonnets Shakespeare tells of a lover's longings, likening them to the fair days of spring and summer, and the sadness of parting and absence like the days of winter. Here is a short verse describing the feelings of December.

How like a winter hath my absence been
From thee, the pleasure of the fleeting year!
What freezings have I felt, what dark days seen!
What old December's bareness everywhere!
And yet this time remov'd was summer's time,
The teeming autumn, big with rich increase,
Bearing the wanton burdon of the prime . . .

The Order of Christmas Continued

From Dugdale's Origines Juridiciales

This is a continuation of the 'Order of Christmas' from Dugdale's Origines Juridiciales; the following days describe the more riotous 'revells' of Shakespeare's England. Included are some notes as to the origins and meanings of the customs.

St. John's Day – About seaven of the clock in the morning, the Lord of Misrule is abroad, and if he lacks any Officer or Attendant, he repaireth to their Chambers, and compelleth them to attend in person upon him after

Service in the Church, to Breakfast, with Brawn, Mustard and Malmsey. After Breakfast ended, his Lordship's power is in suspense, until his personal presence at night; and then his power is most potent.

After the second course (of Dinner), the King's Searjant, orator-like, declareth the disorder of the Constable-Marshall, and the Common Searjant; who defendeth himself and Constable-Marshall, with words of great efficacy. Hereto the King's Searjant replyeth. They rejoyn etc. and who so is found faulty is committed to the Tower etc.

This ceremony follows an ancient pre-Christian custom of electing a scapegoat as 'King', allowing him all honours, then sacrificing him, in the belief that in dying with all honours he is taking all the ills of the people with him. In Shakespeare's time, the 'king' or in this case, the Constable-Marshall, is given a mock trial, and committed to the Tower, but is not really sent there but to the tower 'corner' where stand the four model Tower Bearers.

If any officer be found absent from Dinner or Supper; if it be complained of, he that sitteth in his place is adjudged to have like punishment as the Officer should have been present: and then withall he is enjoyned to supply the office of the true absent Officer, in all pointe. If any Offender escape from the Lieutenant into the Butry, and bring into the Hall a Manchet of Bread upon the point of a Knife, he is pardoned: for the Buttry in that case is Sanctuary. After Cheese is served to the Table not any is commanded to sing.

Childermas Day [Now known as Holy Innocents].

In the Morning, as afore, the Hall is served; saving that the Sewer, Carver, and Cup-Bearer, do not attend any Service. Also like Ceremony at Supper.

New Year's Eve – At Breakfast, Brawn, Mustard & Malmsey. At Dinner, Roast Beef, Venison Pasties, with like solemnities as afore. And at Supper, Mutton, and Hens roasted.

New Year's Day – In the morning, Breakfast as formerly. At Dinner, like solemnity as at Christmas Eve.

From this we see that the present custom of New Year is newer than that observed in Shakespeare's time.

The Banquetting Night.

This is most likely to have been the eve of Twelfth Day, which was the traditional time for the activities which are following described. While many of Shakespeare's plays were performed on the other days of Christmas, notably St Stephen's Day, which we now call 'Boxing Day', and Holy

A Falstaffian character plays to a courtyard audience in Shakespeare's England.

Innocent's Day, the traditional time, when most of his plays were probably performed, was in fact Twelfth Eve. Plays, particularly the Comedies, were most popular during the reign of Queen Elizabeth, while King James who followed her preferred the Masques.

It is proper to the Butlers Office to give warning to every House of Court, of this Banquet; to the end that they, and the Innes of Chancery, be invited thereto to see a Play and Mask. The Hall is to be furnished with Scaffolds to sit on, for Ladies to behold the Sports, on each side. Which ended, the Ladies are to be brought into the Library, unto the Banquet there; and a table is to be covered and furnished with all Banquetting Dishes, for the Lord Chancellor, in the Hall; where he is to call to him the Ancients of the other Houses, as many as may be on one side of the Table. The Banquet is to be served by the Gentlemen of the House.

The Marshall and Steward are to come before the Lord Chancellor's mess. The Butlers for Christmas must serve Wine; and the Butlers of the House Beer and Ale, etc. When the Banquet is ended, then cometh into the Hall the Constable-Marshall, fairly mounted on his Mule; and deviseth some Sport for passing away the rest of the Night.

Twelfth Day – At Breakfast, Brawn, Mustard and Malmsey, after Morning Prayer ended. And at Dinner, the Hall is to be served as upon St. John's Day.

'The Burning Babe'

F a t h e r   R o b e r t   S o u t h w e l l ,   m a r t y r

Religious persecution, begun in Henry VIII's reign, was at its height in the years during Shakespeare's life. Elizabeth, otherwise so sensible and just in her preoccupation with the healthy and fair living of her people, was remarkably harsh concerning religion. Robert Southwell was born four years before Shakespeare and was sent abroad at an early age to be educated. At the age of twenty-four he came back to England as a priest ministering to the persecuted Catholics who were not allowed to practise

their religion under pain of death. Southwell found time to write a number of poems before he was caught, tortured and executed at Tyburn on 21 February 1595, aged only thirty-two years. 'The Burning Babe' was written during his last Christmas/winter season in prison, 1594–5, as part of a group of poems called 'Moeoniae'. It was a theological poem which was later praised by Ben Jonson, who said that he would have been content to destroy many of his own writings if he had written 'The Burning Babe'. Southwell also wrote 'New Heaven, New War', a long poem from which Benjamin Britten took several verses to set to music:

> This little Babe, so few days old
> Is come to rifle Satans fold.
> All Hell doth at His presence quake,
> Though he himself from cold do shake.

Father Southwell's martyrdom was notorious in London that year and Shakespeare would certainly have been familiar with his poems, the story behind the man and the news of his execution. Many poets and

'The Burning Babe' by Walter Crane (1871).

*playwrights of the day made comment about the worth of the man. We
have no record that Shakespeare was one of them, but perhaps as his
contemporaries and friends spoke of Southwell with affection,
Shakespeare did too!*

As I in a hoary Winter's night stood shivering in the snow,
Surprised I was with sudden heat which made my heart to glow;
And lifting up a fearful eye to view what fire was near,
A pretty Babe all burning bright did in the air appear.
As though his floods should quench his flames with what His tears were fed;
Alas, quoth He, but newly born in fiery heats I fry,
Yet none approach to warm their hearts or feel my fire but I.
My faultless breast the furnace is, the fuel is wounding thorns,
Love is the fire, and sighs the smoke, the ashes shame and scorns;
The fuel Justice layeth on, and Mercy blows the coals;
The metal in this furnace wrought are men's defiled souls
For which, as now on fire I am, to work them to their good,
So will I melt into a bath, to wash them in my blood
With this, He vanished, out of sight, and swiftly shrunk away
And straight I called unto mind that this was Christmas Day.

Olde Father Christmas

A SECOND EXTRACT FROM CHRISTMAS UNDER QUEEN ELIZABETH

E s m e   S t u a r t

*This is a description of that hoary old gent as he appeared in
Shakespeare's England, extracted from* Christmas under Queen
Elizabeth *by Esme Stuart (1865). This novel is based around the
Christmas preparations in Elizabethan England, and this piece describes
the belief in old Father Christmas, and the superstition that he brought*

the snow with a chuckling shake of his beard, and how in later times his tears of loneliness caused rainy Christmases! The role of the Elizabethan housewife and the disapproval of the old Puritan tutor for the coming celebrations are also related here.

Surely, in those olden days old Father Christmas was more of a smiling old man than he now appears to us! I fear we have offended him by taking too little notice of him. He has now folded his arms, and as he shakes his head reproachfully, he says, 'Yes, yes; it's all very well for you: you say you are too busy now to attend to me. I am a jolly old fellow doubtless, but really, I am rather too much of a good thing. They did not say so in the year 1570 – oh no! Do you know what they did when I was walking slowly toward them? Oh no! of course you don't, because you have never taken the trouble to inquire. But I won't tell you. Only one thing will I say: that they enjoyed my company a great deal more in those days than you do now. I made myself a great deal more amusing. Ah! ah! my old sides shake to think of it. And what snow-storms I brought along with my white locks. Ah! Ah! when I laughed and shook my hoary head, the earth became white, and the

Olde Father Christmas, from an 1860s' Christmas card.

72

ice spread itself over the water, and the icicles got blue noses, and my fingers made everything look like frosted silver when I touched them accidentally. Ah! Ah! Ah! I was a jolly boy then, but now well well, it's quite altered. People do not believe I can do this anymore. I can't expect you young people who have smoky trains, and I don't know how many posts in the day, to care whether I stay long with you or not. I hear you say quite sadly, "Dear me! There's Christmas coming again; it seems but yesterday since he was here last". The folks in 1570 said quite otherwise. Ah me! it is hard when old people have to be put away on the shelf; but it's the way of the world;' and the old gentleman melts into tears; and this is the reason we often have a mild and wet Christmas.

But in the time of good Queen Bess, Father Christmas was a welcome guest, and his approach was hailed with delight and joy. And nowhere did he receive more greetings than at Sandy's Hollow. Perhaps Dame Pennyfeather was the only one who did not altogether expect him with unbounded pleasure, for her mind was weighed down by the beef and venison which would have been provided. Then the beer! What would her husband say if every man on the premises had not enough – and more than enough – to drink; so she must see that there was plenty brewed; and there must be the best malt put in, for the labourer knows what good beer is as well, nay, better than his superiors.

There was also some present to be provided for each family, and her own household was not satisfied unless a gift was ready for them on Christmas Eve. Dame Pennyfeather was, however, quite equal to the occasion. Her daughter Eve wished many times in the morning that her duties were only made up of looking after the household. She could not see that going to visit the dairy, and ordering the maids, could even be considered as duties . . .

'What has taken away your spirits, good sir?' (asked Annys of Pastor Hapgood) about a week before Christmas.

'I would not burden a young heart with the troubles of one who is not far off from his grave, but e'en you must know that we live in sad times, and wickedness is rampant.'

On Christmas Eve, Ben and his sister were to have a fortnight's holiday, and it was with no little glee that they found the time drawing near. Instead of being more attentive they were less so, and this circumstance did not help to smooth the brow of the weary pastor.

Tamora

FROM *TITUS ANDRONICUS*

William Shakespeare

In Titus Andronicus *Shakespeare made this oblique reference to mistletoe.*

. . . Had I not reason, think you, to look pale?
These two have tied me hither to this place,
A barren detested vale you see it is;
The trees, though summer, yet forlorn and lean,
O'ercome with Moss, and baleful Mistletoe.

How to Make Benicryz

ADAPTED FROM THE ORIGINAL RECIPE

Maria Hubert

Benicryz, or 'benicrz' as I have also seen it spelled, is a delicious mini doughnut-type of dessert, which was popular throughout the seventeenth century and probably earlier. There are similar street sweets served in Spain called Churros and Roscos – the latter containing sherry – which were originally served at the great feasts, including the Feast of Holy Cross. I do not profess to know the origin of the name Benicrz, but 'Beni' could be a corruption of the Spanish or Latin words for 'good' and 'crz' could possibly be a corruption of 'cruz', or 'cross'. The recipe appears in several manuscripts and printed cookery books of the late sixteenth and seventeenth centuries. It was a popular snack at the street fairs of Elizabethan and Jacobean England, when one could buy a

portion freshly fried to eat hot. Perhaps it may have been one of the sweets served to play-goers. The archaic language of the original recipe has been modernized here so that readers who wish to try the recipe can do so more easily!

Take six tablespoonfuls of flour (plain); grate a little nutmeg into it and a pinch of salt, put in a tablespoonful of sweet sherry, and mix it with milk, as thick as for pancakes. Leave for a few minutes while you melt butter into a pan (non-stick for best results today), and pour just enough of the mixture to make a very thin pancake. Let it set but not brown.

When they are all made thus, our seventeenth-century housewife would beat them in a mortar (perhaps a mixer, or better still a food processor, would be today's equivalent), adding six eggs, one at a time.

Heat beef suet (or oil) in a large deep pan and put in a knife's blade of the mixture at a time to fry quickly. Now we may quote from our original recipe for the authentic finale:

When lightly browned take them out of the liquid with a slice and set them in a cullender before the fire (to keepe warme and drain off of the fat). The quicker you serve them the better, grate sugar over them very thick and serve them up.

Christmas Day in the Evening

A FURTHER EXTRACT FROM *CHRISTMAS UNDER QUEEN ELIZABETH*

Esme Stuart

In this extract the family settle down determined to enjoy their Christmas Day despite the fire from the night before. Here all the customs of Christmas that Shakespeare would have known within his

own family are described picturesquely: the churchgoing, the 'luck' gift of a holly sprig, the entry of Father Christmas and the Boar's Head, and ending with the visits to the poor and sick.

'A happy Christmas to ye!' To be sure, why should anyone be sad on such a day? Poor and rich, high and low, all share in the highest sense that happiness, so that there is no mockery in the good yeoman's words as he walks round to all his cottages, saying in his own cheery voice, 'A merry Christmas to you!'

First, there is the churchgoing. All the family go that day, even the twins, for all house-work has been prepared beforehand. Then when they return once more, Ben, who has run on in front, meets them at the door, shouting and singing till his throat is hoarse, and presents each one with an immense piece of Holly. Then what a bustle there is, what a settling of plates, what a shouting for Annys and Jacob! who are at last discovered bending over an old pot where an orphine once grew. Never mind, Annys had watered that pot well with her tears, and foolish Jacob was going to keep it as a relic.

'Dear me! Dear me!' says old Father Christmas, laughing very loud, 'how foolish lovers can be, to be sure; nearly as foolish as poor old Father Christmas himself; however, everyone has their turn, so that makes it even. Come now, boys, give me room; I am the herald of the wonderful Boar's Head!' Then follows a long procession of men-servants and maid-servants, in the midst of which may be seen the boar's head all decorated with holly, and a grim smile illuminating his face. There are few who can smile at their own death, but then few have such a fuss made over them. As the boar is placed on the table Maurice gets up and sings in his full sweet tones –

> Caput Apri defero
> Reddens laudes Domino.
>
> The Boar's Head in hand bear I
> With Garlands Gay and Rosemary;
> I pray you all sing merrily,
> Qui estis in convivio.
>
> The Boar's Head I understand
> Is the chief service in this land;

Look wherever it be fande
Servite cum canto.

Be glad, Lords, both more and lasse,
For this hath ordained our steward
To cheer you all this Christ-e-masse
The Boar's Head with the Mustarde!

After which the family begin the real business of eating. No tasting of morsels in those days; people would have been ashamed of having ten courses handed round and 'just touching' say, five of them. No, no, no, they had a dinner and they made a dinner, and that is why the brave English could fight those poor Spaniards and snap their fingers at the Armada. I will not make your mouths water with the descriptions of that dinner; suffice to say it was a very good one, and that the sight of the happy faces round the board was a feast in itself. I must proceed with my story. Many neighbours had come on this Christmas Day to see the burnt wing of Master Pennyfeather's house, and many were the inquiries into the cause of the conflagration. . . . These wonderings were brought to a close by the yeoman saying in his usual happy, good-natured voice,

The Boar's Head, an anonymous picture from the eighteenth century.

Refreshments for the fiddlers, from Christmas Under Queen Elizabeth *(illustration by Stacy Marks, ARA).*

'Come, neighbours, let us amuse ourselves. Here come the fiddlers, and here is the hall. I must first introduce you to my future son-in-law, whose gallant conduct is in everyone's mouth. His left arm, you see, is useless; but we neighbours shall watch and see whether he will not manage to foot it with Annys. Come, Jacob, take her hand and open the Ball!'

No sooner said than done, and Jacob's whole countenance seemed changed by happiness. What will not joy accomplish in the beautifying of the face? Joy just touches with soft fingers the eyes, and at once they become radiant and beautiful; next he kisses the mouth, and the curves seem to alter and appear lovely. Nay, joy has sometimes pressed his fingers into some soft cheek and left there a dimple: but sometimes he does all this and then flies away, saying, 'I only wanted to show you what I was like you see, I cannot stay with you today; perhaps some other day I will see you again, but who knows?' Ah! who knows indeed if the joys of the days that are no more will ever return?

The dance had begun at two o'clock in the afternoon, for late balls were not in fashion just then.

About half-past-four, when Annys had sunk into a chair quite tired out with dancing and happiness, some loud and unmusical voices were heard singing outside. It was growing dusk, and the sounds agreed well with the hour.

'Ah! Chance has brought us some stray carol singers,' remarked Jacob, 'but they are behindhand.'

'Nay, they are but strolling minstrels; I will go and offer them some of our new brew; it is first rate, some say. Ah, Jacob! I feel as if I could make everyone happy as I am myself. This time on Saturday that dreadful kinsman of ours was sitting by me, but I remember not one word he said!'

'Thou hast a short memory my Annys, perhaps thou hast forgotten what I told thee on the bowling green?'

'No, no, of that converse I remember every word. But I had nearly forgotten the singers;' and snatching up a large jug of beer and a tumbler, Annys hurried to the door; at once the sound of voices and flutes ceased. Annys beheld two men and a boy, who looked with longing eyes at the windows where the merry party were seated. One of the three was an old red faced peasant, who, if he could sing at all, certainly could make no heavenly music. As soon as he saw Annys, he tucked his fiddle under his arm, and gazed with greedy eyes at the tumbler. The other man was tall and strong, looking far too hale for a man to turn beggar, for these wandering minstrels were not much better. The lad had a round, good-humoured face, but evidently did not find playing the flute a very agreeable Christmas Day occupation.

'It is most too chilly for you, good folk,' said Annys kindly, as she poured out the beer, 'will you not enter a while?'

'Nay, thank-you,' answered the sturdy man somewhat shortly, then added, 'We come on an errand to Mistress Annys Pennyfeather.'

'To me?' cried Annys; 'who then sent you?'

'As we passed a cottage some fifteen minutes walk from here, a woman came hurriedly out and begged us if we were passing Master Pennyfeather's house to call, and ask Mistress Annys, of her charity to hasten thither, for her child was sore taken with some complaint, of which she described the symptoms' . . . Annys hastened away, and a few minutes after Jacob saw her trip off on her deed of charity.

Mysteries, Minstrels & Puppets

THE STREET PLAYS OF SHAKESPEARE'S TIME WITH 'A HYMN OF THE NATIVITY SUNG BY THE SHEPHERDS' BY RICHARD CRASHAW

The mystery plays known to Shakespeare were not the same as those we are familiar with today. In Elizabethan England a mystery was a telling of one of the stories from the Bible. These were originally performed by the guilds, who were most solicitous of their own parts, and they were performed on 'floats', movable carts, which were set up in different parts of the town. The popular scene of the Massacre of the Holy Innocents in the mystery plays from Coventry, which was very close to Stratford, was the prerogative of the Shearers and Taylors Guild.

These plays were also performed at fairs by travelling showmen, who used puppets, a custom which lasted well into the twentieth century in parts of Europe, notably Italy and Poland. Such sights were also familiar to the Bard who refers to them briefly in The Winter's Tale.

The third group to work with the mysteries were the minstrels and the poets. They would write verses with individual parts to be sung to an audience, usually of a house party. The shepherds were the most popular character for this entertainment, and such songs could be performed by invitation or by gatecrashing – as did Henry VIII in Shakespeare's play of the same name, when Henry and a group of maskers gatecrash Wolsey's house party, dressed as shepherds (Act I, sc. iv).

The following is a part song of the shepherds written by Richard Crashaw, 1612–49. Born of Puritan parents, he was educated at Charterhouse and Cambridge and became a Catholic in the middle years of his short life.

The Shepherds, a photogravure by Wright & Stokes reproduced in The Christmas Book of Songs *(1910).*

A HYMN OF THE NATIVITY SUNG BY THE SHEPHERDS

Come, we shepherds whose blest sight
Hath met Love's noon in Nature's night;
Come, lift we up our loftier song,
And wake the sun that lies too long.
To all our world of well-stol'n joy

He slept, and dreamt of no such thing,
While we found out Heaven's fairer eye,
And kiss'd the cradle of our King;
Tell him he rises now too late
To show us aught worth looking at.

Tell him we now can show him more
Than he e'er showed a mortal sight,
Than he himself e'er saw before,
Which to be seen needs not his light:
Tell him, Tityrus, where thou' hast been,
Tell him Thyrsis, what thou hast seen.

TITYRUS:
Gloomy night embraced the place
Where the noble infant lay;
The babe look'd up and showed his face;
In spite of darkness it was day.
It was Thy day, sweet, and did rise,
Not from the East but from thy eyes.
CHORUS: It was Thy day, sweet . . .

THYRSIS:
Winter chid aloft, and sent
The angry North to wage his wars:
The North forgot his fierce intent,
And left perfumes instead of scars.
By those sweet eyes' persuasive powers,
Where he meant frosts he scattered flowers.
CHORUS: By those sweet eyes' . . .

BOTH:
We saw Thee in Thy balmy nest,
Young dawn of our eternal day;
We saw Thine eyes break from the East,
And chase the trembling shades away:
We saw Thee, and we blest the sight,
We saw Thee by Thine own sweet light.
CHORUS: We see Thee, . . .

TITYRUS:
Poor world said I, what wilt thou do
To Entertain this starry stranger?
Is this the best thou can'st bestow –
A cold and not too cleanly manger?
Contend, the powers of heaven and earth,
To fit a bed for this huge birth.
CHORUS: Contend, the powers . . .

THYRSIS:
Proud world, said I, cease your contest,
And let the mighty babe alone,
The phoenix builds the phoenix's nest,
Love's architecture is His own.
The babe, whose birth embraves this morn,
Made His own bed e'er He was born.
CHORUS: The babe, whose birth . . .

TITYRUS:
I saw the curls drops, soft and slow,
Come hovering o'er the place's head,
Off'ring their whitest sheets of snow,
To furnish the fair infant's bed.
Forbear, said I be not too bold,
Your fleece is white, but 'tis too cold.
CHORUS: Forbear, said I . . .

THYRSIS:
I saw the obsequious seraphim
Their rosy fleece of fire bestow,
For well they now can spare their wings
Since Heaven itself lies here below.
Well done, said I: but are you sure
Your down soft warm, will pass for pure?
CHORUS: Well done, said I . . .

BOTH:
No, no, your King's not yet to seek
Where to repose His royal head;

See, see how soon His new-bloom'd cheek
'Twixt mother's breasts is gone to bed.
Sweet choice, said we, no way but so,
Not to lie cold, yet sleep in snow!
CHORUS: Sweet choice . . .

FULL CHORUS:
Welcome all wonders in one sight!
Eternity shut in a span!
Summer in winter! Day in night!

CHORUS:
Heaven in earth! and God in man!
Great little one, whose all-embracing birth
Lifts earth to heaven, stoops heaven to earth!

To Thee meek Majesty, soft King
Of simple graces and sweet loves!
Each of us his lamb will bring
Each his pair of silver doves!
At last, in fire of Thy fair eyes,
Ourselves become our own best sacrifice.

Shakespeare's Christmas Dinner

AND CHRISTMAS HUSBANDLY FARE BY THOMAS TUSSER

*What festive fare would Shakespeare have enjoyed, as a boy growing up
in Stratford-upon-Avon and as a man, when many of his Christmases
were spent in London entertaining the Queen and her royal court with
one of his plays such as* Measure for Measure, *which was first performed*

at court on 26 December 1604. Doubtless he would have enjoyed more elegant food than his wife would have provided, even at the height of his popularity. Christmas fare tended to be as varied then as it is now. Some families would have eaten the good roast beef of old England, others would have preferred brawn. If you were at Oxford University, you would have feasted on boar's head with mustard, of which brawn, made from the meat of a pig's head, is a descendant. A few had already succumbed to the new fashionable meat recently brought from the Americas and said to be the favourite Christmas dish of Queen Elizabeth I – the turkey. Mince pies were made with real meat, usually shredded tongue, and the spices were symbolic of the Holy Land, where Jesus was born. The original spices were brought back by crusader knights.

The following poem is by Thomas Tusser, a poet who was already an elderly man when Shakespeare was born. Tusser was a great observer and recorder of the domestic and the natural world around him, and in Christmas Husbandly Fare, *written in the late sixteenth century, he gives an account of what would have been served in a household such at that in which young Will Shakespeare grew up:*

Bringing the Christmas pie to the table, from 'A Christmas Carroll' (illustration by Frank Merrill, 1895).

Good Husband and Housewife, now chiefly be glad
Things handsome to have, as they ought to be had,
They both do provide against Christmas do come,
To welcome their neighbour, good cheer to have some;
Good bread and good drink, a good fire in the hall,
Brawn pudding and souse, and good mustard withal;
Beef, mutton, and pork, shred pies of the best,
Pig, veal, goose, and capon, and turkey well dress'd;
Cheese, apples, and nuts, jolly carols to hear,
As then in the country is counted good cheer.

What cost to good husband is any of this,
Good household provision only it is;
Of other the like I do leave out a many,
That costeth the husbandman never a penny.

*A very descriptive account of what was considered a 'moderate'
dinner of the time is also found in a book on housewifery of the time:*

There should be full sixteen dishes at table; that is, dishes of meat
that are of substance, and not empty or for show – as thus, for
example; first, a shield of Brawne with Mustarde; secondly a boyl'd
Capon; thirdly, a boyl'd piece of Beef; fourthly, a Chine of Beef, rosted;
fifthly, a neat's Tongue, rosted; sixthly, a Pig, rosted; seventhly,
Chewets, baked; eighthly, a Goose rosted; ninethly, a Swan, rosted;
tenthly, a Turkie, rosted; the eleventh, a haunch of Venison, rosted; the
twelfth, a pasty of Venison; the thirteenth, a Kid, with a pudding in the
belly; the fourteenth, an Olive-pye; the fifteenth, a couple of Capons;
the sixteenth, a Custard, or Dowsetts.

Now to these full dishes may be added sallets, fricases, quelque
choses, and devised paste, as many dishes more, which make the full
service no less than two and thirty dishes; which is as many as can
conveniently stand on one table, and in one messe. And after this
manner you may proportion both your second and third courses,
holding fulness on one half of the dishes, and show on the other; which
will be both frugal in the splendour, contentment to the guest, and
much pleasure and delight to the beholder.

A Receipt for a Bean Cake

A SIXTEENTH-CENTURY RECIPE FOR A TWELFTH NIGHT CAKE

This is the late sixteenth-century recipe for a cake for Twelfth Night, such as was made by housewives in Shakespeare's time. There are no records of what Shakespeare's mother, Mary Arden, or his wife, Anne, would have produced for Christmas, but as this recipe was a popular one, it is conceivable that they might have made it. Bean cake appears to have been a kind of gingerbread, and was called peppercake in the Northern counties. It was distinct from Twelfth cake, which was a rich fruit cake, iced and decorated in a manner similar to that of Christmas cake, which is its descendant.

In later years, without its bean, but served with a thin slice of cheese, bean cake used to be given to children and callers at Christmas time, and the following verse is associated with the cake:

A Little bit of Peppercake,
A little bit of cheese,
A cup of cold water
And a penny if you please.

In the recipe for the bean cake you can omit the pearl ash if you wish; it adds little to the flavour really, but for those who wish to use it it can generally be purchased in small quantities from most dispensing chemists.

Ingredients:

1 lb plain flour
1 teaspoon pearl ash melted in a
  little lukewarm milk
1 oz powdered cloves
1 lb black treacle

1 teaspoon ground white pepper
1 teaspoon ground ginger
1 lb butter
5 beaten eggs

Mix all ingredients together – you can use a mixer. You will find it easier if you melt the treacle with the butter and add to the flour and spices and then add the eggs, in that order. Line baking tins or cake tins with baking parchment and bake in a moderate oven (about 160°C for electric) for about two hours.

This is a typical old recipe to make one very large cake. If you use smaller tins, reduce the baking time accordingly. The usual cake tests apply, springs back when pressed. Allow to go cold, and slice thinly. Nice spread with butter, marmalade, or the traditional cheese.

If you are making a bean cake, wrap the dried bean (I use dried butter beans) in parchment and put into the dough. Slice the cake for as many guests as will be eating it, and the winner of the bean either becomes your King/Queen for the party, or you can have a small 'unisex' gift ready to bestow!

On Flapdragon

A SUMMARY OF ACCOUNTS OF THE ANCIENT GAME QUOTED BY SHAKESPEARE

Various accounts of the ancient game of Snapdragon, which has been a Christmas pastime certainly from medieval times – or earlier if we are to believe the players in Lingua *– to the present. Shakespeare was certainly familiar with it, for he brings it into two of his plays; here is how it was acknowledged in Shakespeare's day:*

From the play LINGUA, 1607.

MEMORY: O I remember this dish well, it was first invented by Pluto, to intertaine Proserpina withall.
PHANTASTES: – I thinke not, Memory, for when Heracles had kild the flaming dragon of Hesperdia with the Apples of that Orchard he made this fiery meate; in memory whereof hee named it Snapdragon.

Henry IV, Part II, Act II, sc. iv, Falstaff says that the Prince likes Poins because he:

'. . . plays at quoits well, eats conger and fennel and drinks off candles's ends for flap-dragons . . .'

Can he possibly be referring to the West Country custom, which was not quite the same as the fruit and brandy Snapdragon, in which a lighted candle was placed in a cup of cider or ale and the player had to drink the ale without burning his face? And again the Bard makes reference to the sport in Love's Labour's Lost *(Act V, sc. i), when Costard, upon encountering a group who are arguing at length, says to Moth, his companion:*

'. . . I marvel thy master has not eaten thee for a word; for thou art not so long, by the head as honorificabilitudinitatibus: thou are easier swallowed than a flap-dragon'.

John Ashton, writing of the Elizabethan sport in 1893, describes it as:

. . . A kind of game, in which Brandy is poured over a large dish of raisins, and then set alight. The object is to snatch the raisins out of the flames and devour them without burning oneself. This can be managed by sharply seizing them and shutting the mouth at once. It is suggested that the name is derived from the German Snappes, 'spirit' and Drache 'Dragon'.

'Here he comes with flaming bowl, Snip, Snap, Dragon!', from Pantalogia (1813).

Sandys, writing in the early 1800s, also makes reference to Shakespeare and Flapdragon:

In juvenile parties, Snap-Dragon, throwing its mysterious and witchlike hue over the faces of the bystanders. Not Poin's who swallowed down candle ends for flap-dragons; but the veritable Malaga fruit, carolling away in the frolicsome spirit, burning the fingers but rejoicing the palate of the adventurous youth, and half frightened little maiden reveller. The custom is old, but not quite so old as stated in the curious play 'Lingua' by the performance of one character, wherein – Tactus – Oliver Cromwell is said to have had his first dream of ambition.

The Elizabethan love of forfeits and gambling games made Snapdragon, or Flapdragon, a most popular pastime. And several people wrote on its merits or otherwise, and described methods for achieving success. Elizabethan advice repeated in 'Pantalogia' (1813) advised the 'gamsters' thus:

Set fire to the warm brandy in an earthenware bowl, and throw raisins into it. Those who are unused to this sport are afraid to pluck out the fruit, but the raisins may be safely snatched out by a quick motion and put blazing into the mouth which being closed, the fire is at once extinguished. The game requires both courage and rapidity of action, and a good deal of merriment is caused by the unsuccessful efforts of competitors for the raisins in the flaming bowl.

The following verse was traditionally sung by onlookers while the foolhardy tried their luck and their fingers in the dish of flaming fruit.

> Here he comes with flaming Bowle,
> Don't he mean to take hys tolle,
> Snip! Snap! Dragon!

> Take care you don't take too much,
> Be not greedy in your clutch,
> Snip! Snap! Dragon!

> With his blue and lappinge Tongue,
> Many of you will bee stung,
> Snip! Snap! Dragon!

For he snaps at alle that comes,
Snatching at his feast of Plums,
Snip! Snap! Dragon!

But Olde Christmasse makes hym come
Though he lookes so fee! fa! fum!
Snip! Snap! Dragon!

Don't 'ee feare him, bee but bold
Out he goes, his flames are colde,
Snip! Snap! Dragon!

An 1860s' Christmas card depicting the game of Snapdragon.

The Holy Bough and Divers Customs Explained

CHRISTMAS CUSTOMS AND PRACTICES IN SHAKESPEARE'S ENGLAND

M a r i a   H u b e r t

The customs of old England were rather different to those today. They were all vestiges of more ancient and often pre-Christian customs which had been adapted by the Church in the face of the obstinacy of the unconverted peoples of Britain when faced with the early missionaries of

St Gregory. He told his missionaries not to throw out 'that which is good, but adapt it. If they decorate their temples to the Sun God, let them continue to do it in honour of the Son of God'. Thus many of the customs were given a new meaning to encourage people to turn to Christianity. After the Reformation, many of the customs fell into disuse, and those which did continue in small hidden pockets of Britain, hidden away from Parliamentary eyes, or those which were later revived, had all but lost their meanings. Below a few of the interesting customs which were prevalent in Shakespeare's day are described.

Long before the Christmas tree had come to Britain from Central Europe, the custom of hanging a bough of evergreens was popular. This custom also came from overseas, but reached our shores much earlier than the tree. It was known in the thirteenth century and possibly earlier, reaching its height of popularity in Elizabethan times. It is possible that the Shakespeares may have had such a bough over their door, but not very probable, as the restrictions imposed by the Crown on the old 'Roman' customs was already beginning to bite by the time Shakespeare was a boy of about seven. Certainly both of his parents would have been familiar with the custom, particularly his mother who came from the ancient and wealthy Ardens, whose family was originally Norman.

The Holy Bough was originally a 'Sacramental', that is, a custom which was encouraged by the Church which in turn bestowed a blessing on those practising the custom. It consisted of a double hoop of willow or hazel, around which were garlanded and plaited evergreens – ivy, bay, rosemary, holly, and mistletoe – anything, in fact, which was green and available. On to this was then tied any fancy piece available – ribbons, pretty baubles, glass jewellery baubles in particular and occasionally gilded nuts if the household were wealthy enough, gilded nutmegs and cinnamon sticks. Seedheads and dried flowers and grasses, cereal stems such as wheat or corn, and lavender were also saved during the summer for this purpose.

A base made either from plaited and woven natural materials, or from wood, was placed in the middle and secured at the lower end of the hoop and on to this was put a representation of the Holy Family, sometimes just a babe in a crib, sometimes the whole group. These could be crudely whittled, made from wax or carefully carved, depending on the wealth or skills of the household. Some, by the time of Shakespeare, were dressed. There is a reference to a 'wooden doll in clouts' in *The Popish Kingdom* by Barnaby

Googe (1570) being placed on the altar. This custom of dressing a carved image as the Christchild acted as a visual 'aid' to understanding Christmas for a largly illiterate populace and was extremely popular at this time.

Having thus dressed their boughs, the family would then hang them on a hook just over the outer door, or somewhere close to the threshold of the house. There, in pre-Reformation times, they would be blessed by the parish priest, who would make a special trip around his parish to perform this action. This bestowed a blessing upon the household as well. Anyone who visited the house during the Christmas season, which was the season of peace and goodwill to all men, had to show his or her goodwill with an embrace under this bough, something like the Kiss of Peace in Churches today.

A similar custom was observed between New Year and Epiphany, when the priest would again visit his parish and bless the houses, leaving a chalked cross on the rafters to show that the household was a God-fearing one. Barnaby Googe in *The Popish Kingdom* refers to this custom being performed by the master of the house or another visitor. Sadly by the time he was writing, it had become difficult to have a house blessing by the priest and, unless one had a secret blessing performed by a recusant priest, this was done by members of the family. Sometimes the 'King' bean whose riotous behaviour scandalized Googe so, was a priest in disguise.

The Holy Bough became something of a status symbol among more well-to-do families, each vying with the others to create the costliest and most extravagant bough – somewhat defeating the reasons for the bough in the first place, as the ensuing 'competition' was not always full of goodwill! After the Restoration of course, it became the Holly Bough, or Kissing Bunch, and the Kiss of Peace was reduced to a kiss for a berry under the mistletoe, its origins forgotten.

It was also the custom for the Wassail Virgins to go around to the houses calling blessings upon the household. These were the Vestal Virgins of pre-Christian cultures, who were dedicated to the temples of the old religions. Another version of this custom was the Milly Box maids. 'Milly' is said to be a corruption of 'Maiden's Box' and later 'Milady's Box', referring to the Virgin Mary. It consisted of a box with an interior covered with moss, dried flowers, etc. and in it was a figure to represent the Baby Jesus. The whole was prettily decorated and covered with a 'sacred cloth'. The maids carried it around, singing their Christmas songs, and for an 'offering' they would take off the cloth and let the contents be admired.

Sandys in *Xmas Customs* (1836) states that during Shakespeare's time carolling in the streets was popular. Many groups carolled – the Wassail Virgins, the Milly Maids, the Watchmen, who went around the streets keeping law and order and telling the hour throughout the night. They would sing and were the origin of the Waits or 'Wakemen', who kept vigil through the night.

The Milly Box custom originated, it is thought by scholars, as a devotion to the pagan deity, the baby Dionysus in pre-Christian times. After the Restoration it was just another carolling custom with a 'Pretty Box', which usually, but not always, contained an image of the Baby Jesus.

Shakespeare tells how Autolycus would frequent the fairs and see the puppets performing the mystery plays. These puppets were owned by travelling puppeteers, who would carry their 'theatre' on their backs and tell the stories of the Bible, the 'Mysteries' as they were called, with their puppets at fairs and markets. The practice originated in Europe and then travelled to Britain.

Shakespearean Christmas Gifts

WITH QUOTES FROM *THE WINTER'S TALE* AND THE SEVENTEENTH-CENTURY ACCOUNTS, *NICHOL'S PROGRESSES* AND *ILLUSTRATIONS OF MANNERS & EXPENCES*

It was customary to give New Year gifts in Elizabethan times, although it was not unknown to give one at Christmas itself. One wonders what sort of gifts the Bard would have most liked to receive. A new quill pen perhaps, or a knife to sharpen it, powder to blot his writing, and that scarce and expensive commodity, paper to write on. A pouch for his tobacco, an ounce of some fragrant new variety fresh and pungent, even hose or a ruff or a new cambric shirt would have been typical gifts to

give a gentleman of his tastes and requirements.
In The Winter's Tale *Autolycus, a rogue of a pedlar, comes in singing*
his wares thus:

> Lawn as white as driven snow;
> Cyprus black as e'er was crow;
> Gloves as sweet as damask-roses;
> Masks for faces, and for noses;
> Bugle-bracelet, necklace amber,
> Perfume for a lady's chamber;
> Golden quoifs and stomachers,
> For my lads to give their dears;
> Pins, and poking sticks of steel,
> What maids lack from head to heel;
> Come, buy of me, come; come buy, come buy;
> Buy, lads, or else your lasses cry,
> Come buy.

Clown: If I were not in love with Mopsa, thou shouldst take no money of me; but being enthralled as I am, it will also be to bindage of certain ribands and gloves.

Mopsa (a shepherdess): I was promised them against the feast; but they come not too late now.

[though the feast in this instance is the sheep-shearing feast in spring.]

According to William Sandys there was a distinct difference between
New Year gifts and Christmas boxes.
The difference between New Year gifts and Christmas boxes appears
to be that the former were mutually exchanged, or indeed were
sometimes in the nature of an offering from an inferior to a superior,
who made some acknowledgement in return, while the latter were in the
nature of gratuities from superiors to their dependants. The practice is of
considerable antiquity in this country, and formerly it was customary for
the nobility and persons connected with the court to make presents to
the king, who gave gifts, generally of money or plate in return . . .
Sandys goes on to list at length gifts and costs of presents to various
monarchs, the list of Queen Elizabeth I being of most interest to us here:

Queen Elizabeth I receiving her Christmas gifts, from W. Sandys' Christmastide *(1830).*

. . . Queen Elizabeth expected valuable ones [gifts]. They seem to have been much of the same description every year. The peers spiritual and temporal, ladies, gentlewomen, and officers of the household, etc. gave presents according to their rank and means, of money, rich dresses, jewels, etc.; the physicians and apothecary, boxes of ginger and candy; the cook and other domestics, or officers similar gifts to those hereafter mentioned.

These included such items as a pair of cloth of silver sleeves; collar & ruffs of gold damask embroidered with pearls; sugared fruits; a picture of the Holy Trinity; a fat goose and capon, a pair of oxen (from the cook!) and a box of ginger, nutmegs and sticks of cinnamon.

Mr Sandys' sources, Nichol's Progresses *and* Illustrations of Manners & Expences, *give full accounts of the gifts received in the early years of Shakespeare's life, culminating with a gift from the Christmas Maskers in 1581 – too soon to have been one of Shakespeare's own troupe, though, as he would have been only about seventeen, still at home and not yet married. The gifts are interesting and help to show the reader the domestic spirit of the world in which Shakespeare lived. From it one may surmise that the Queen had a liking for candies and ginger, and that she received gifts from everyone – including her dustman! The list for the year 1577–8 shows:*

Sir Gawen Carewe a smock of camerick, wrought with black silk in the collor and sleves, the square and ruffs wrought with Venice golde, and edged with a small bone lace of Venice gold. Also, by Phillip Sydney, a smock of camerick and a sute of ruffs cutworke with 4oz of spangles.

By Doctor Maister, a pot of grene gynger and other of orenge flowers.

By Smythsonne, Master Cooke, a feyer Marchpane.

By Dudley, Sergeant of the Pastry, a greate pye of Quynses and wardyns guilt. [A gilded pie of quince and plums.]

By Christofer Gyles, Cutler, a meate knyf with a feyer hafte of white bone and a conceyte in it.

By Morgan, Apotticary, thre boxes, one of gynger candy, another of grene gynger and the third orenge candit.

By Smyth, Dustman, two bolts of Camerick.

In 1578–9 the list included 'Morris Watkins, eighteen larkes in a cage'. Also mentioned were gowns, petticoats, kirtles, doublets, mantles, some embroidered with precious stones. Bracelets, jewels and ornaments. The list for 1581–2 is also interesting:

1581–2 Item a juell of golde, being a catt and myce playing with her, garnished with smale dyamondes and perle. Given by Lady Howarde.

Item, a flower of golde, garnished with sparcks of diamonds, rubyes, and ophales, with an agathe of her Majestis phisnamy, and a perle pendante, with devices painted in it. Geven by Eight Maskers in Christmas-weeke.

In 1589 she received a fan of red & white feathers, the handle gold and enamelled with a half moon of mother of pearl, within it sparks of diamonds and a few seed pearls on one side, and a picture of her within that. This came from Sir Francis Drake.

In return the queen gave money gifts, or gold or silver plate.

It was also the custom to send foodstuffs as presents and tenants might give a fat bird, or a cake as their means would allow, to their lord. Neighbours expecting an invitation to the party at the 'big house' would send anything from preserves, fruit, pies and cakes, eggs and cheeses, spices, meats and brawns. But from most of the records available, gifts were given, at this level anyway, with the hope of a return – money or gold from the monarch, an invitation from the local lord of the manor – or as a bribe, such as the gloves lined with 'angels' (money), given to Sir Thomas More when he was chancellor. It is reported that he graciously kept the gloves but returned the 'linings'. Sandys comments on this.

Formerly tenants used to make presents at this time to their landlords, frequently a capon, or something of similar value. The following is a list of food gifts sent to a landlord at Wootton by his tenants and neighbours:

'Two sides of Venison, two half brawns, three pigs, ninety capons, five geese, six turkeys, four rabbits, eight partridges, two pullets, five sugar loaves, half a pound of nutmegs, one basket of apples and eggs, three baskets of apples, two baskets of pears.'

Ceremonies for Christmas

AN ACCOUNT IN VERSE OF THE CUSTOMS FOR THE TWELVE DAYS OF CHRISTMAS

R o b e r t   H e r r i c k

Robert Herrick was born in the period when Shakespeare was beginning to gain acclaim as a playwright rather than as an actor. Born to a wealthy goldsmith's family in London, as a boy he would have been undoubtedly familiar with the name of the great Bard, if not his works.

He moved back to his father's old county of Leicestershire to be apprenticed to his uncle, another goldsmith, who was knighted in 1605, and being accepted at court may well have attended some of the plays by Shakespeare put on for the Queen. Robert then went to Cambridge and eventually was ordained into the established English Church. Perhaps because of the resistance to folk culture by the Puritans, Robert developed a great interest in the old traditions of his early family days before his father died when, under Queen Elizabeth, Christmas retained its older customs and developed some new, elaborate ones too.

Hesperides was an outlet for his love of the old Christmas traditions and, together with his other seasonal verses, provides one of the most complete records of Christmas in Shakespearean England.

CHRISTMAS EVE

Come, Bring with a noise, my merry,
   merry, boys,
The Christmas Log to the Firing;
While my good Dame, she, bids you
   all be free,
And drink to your heart's desiring.

With the last year's Brand light the
   new block, and
For good success in his spending
On your psalteries play, that sweet
   luck may
Come while the log is a-teending.

Drink now the strong Beer, cut the
   white loaf here;
While the meat is a-shredding for the
   rare mince-pie,
And the plums stand by
To fill the Paste that's a-kneading.

'Come bring with a noise my merry boys the Christmas log to the firing'. A photogravure by Wright & Stokes from about 1910.

Come guard this night the Christmas-pie,
That the thief, though ne'er so sly,
With his flesh-hooks, don't come nigh
To catch it.

From him, who all alone sits there,
Having his eyes still in his ear,
And a deal of nightly fear,
To watch it.

The following was a warning to the maids that, according to
superstition, a Christmas fire would not light unless all was clean,
including the hands!

TO MAIDS
Wash your hands or else the fire
Will not teend to your desire
Unwashed hands, ye maidens know,
Dead the fire, though ye blow.

The Bell-man grew out of the Watchman, whose job was 365 days a
year and not just for Christmas.

THE BELL-MAN
From noise of scare-fires rest ye free,
From murders, Benedicite!
From all mischances that may fright
Your pleasing slumbers in the night;
Mercy secure ye all, and keep
The goblins from ye, while ye sleep.
Past one o'clock, and almost two,
My Masters all, Good-day to you.

The following extract of a song, written to Sir Simon Steward, tells the
whole Christmas story.

CHRISTMAS SONG

... But here a jolly verse crowned with Ivy and with Holly,
That tells of Winter's tales and mirth,
That milkmaids make about the hearth,
Of Christmas Sports, the Wassail Bowl,
That tost up, after fox-i-th'-hole;
Of Blind Man's Buff, and of the care
That young men have to shoe the Mare;
Of Twelve-tide cakes, of peas and beans,
Wherewith you make those merry scenes,
Whenas ye choose your king and queen,
And cry out, 'Hey for our town green';
Of Ash-heaps, in the which ye use
Husbands and wives by streaks to chose;
Of crackling Laurel, which foresounds
A plentious Harvest to your grounds:
Of these and suchlike things for shift,
We send in stead of New Year's Gift.
Read then, and when your face do shine,
With buxon meat and cap'ring wine,
Remember us, in cups full crowned,
and let our city health go round,
Quite through the young maids and the men
To the ninth number, if not ten.
Until the fired Chestnuts leap
For joy to see the fruits ye reap ...

And let the russet swains the plough
And harrow hang up, resting now;
And to the bagpipe all address,
Till sleep takes place of weariness.
And thus, throughout, with Christmas plays
Frolic the full twelve holidays.

There were two types of wassail. That which one gave to one's own crops and that which the wassailers visited upon the household. The latter is described here.

The Wassailers at the gates (Wright & Stokes, c. 1910).

THE WASSAIL

Give way, give way ye gates and win,
An easy blessing to your bin
And basket, by our entering in.

May both with Manchet stand replete;
Your larders too, so hung with meat,
That though a thousand, thousand eat.

Yet ere twelve moons shall whirl about
Their silv'ry spheres, that none may doubt
But more's sent in than was served out.

Next, may your dairies prosper so
As that your pans no ebb may know;
But if they do, the more to flow.

Like to a solemn sober stream
Bank'd all with lilies, and the cream
Of sweetest cowslips filling them.

Then may your plants be prest with fruit,
Nor bee or hive you have be mute;
But sweetly sounding like a lute.

Next, may your duck and teeming hen
Both to the Cock's tread say Amen;
And for their two eggs render ten.

Last, may your harrows, shears and ploughs,
Your stacks, your stocks, your sweetest mows,
All prosper by our virgin vows.

At New Year it was the traditional time to exchange gifts, rather than at
Christmas itself. Herrick does not only tell us what customs were observed
on this day, but presents them as his gift to the Court at Whitehall.

THE NEW-YEAR'S GIFT

Prepare for songs; He's come, he's come;
And let it be sin here to be dumb,
And not with lutes to fill the room.

Cast Holy-water all about,
And have a care no fire goes out,
But 'cense the porch and place throughout.

The altars all on fire be;
The storax fries, and ye may see
How heart and hand do all agree to make things sweet.

Chorus: Yet all less sweet than He
Bring Him along, most pious priest,

And tell us then, whenas thou seest
His gently gliding, dove-like eyes,
How canst thou this Babe Circumcise?

Chorus: Back, back, again, each thing is done
With zeal alike, as twas begun;
Now singing, homeward let us carry
The Babe unto His mother Mary;
And when we have the Child commended
To the warm bosom, then our rites are ended.

*On the eve of Epiphany the Star-boys visited, representing the
Wise Men following the star to the stable of Bethlehem.*

STAR-SONG

1st traveller: Tell us, thou clear and heavenly tongue,
Where is the Babe but lately sprung?
Lies he the Lily-banks among?

2nd traveller: Or say, if this new Birth of ours
Sleeps, laid within some ark of flowers,
Spangled with dew-light; thou canst clear
All doubts, and manifest the where.

3rd traveller: Declare to us, bright star, if we seek
Him in the morning's blushing cheek,
Or search the beds of spices through,
To find him out.

Star: No, this ye need not do;
But only come and see him rest
A Princely Babe in's Mother's breast.

Chorus: He's seen! He's seen! why then a round,
Lets kiss the sweet and holy ground;
And all rejoice that we have found
A King before conception crown'd.

4th Traveller: Come then, come then, and let us bring
Unto our pretty Twelfth-tide King,
Each one his several offering;

Chorus: And when the night comes, we'll give Him wassailing;
And His treble honours may be seen,
We'll choose Him King and make His Mother, Queen.

On Twelfth Day, the Feast of the Epiphany, religious observances
were made the evening before and then the festivities began.

The Bean King (Wright & Stokes, c. 1910).

TWELFTH NIGHT OR KING & QUEEN

Now, now the mirth comes
With the cake full o' plums,
Where Bean's the king of Sport here;
Beside we must know, the pea also,
Must revel, as queen, in the court here.

Begin then to choose,
This night as ye use,
Who shall for the present, delight here,
Be a king by the lot, And who shall not
Be Twelfth-day queen for the night here.

Which known, let us make
Joy sops, with the cake;
And let not a man then be seen here,
Who unurg'd will not drink to the base from the brink
A health to the queen and the king here.

Next crown the bowl full
With gentle lamb's wool:
Add sugar, nutmeg and ginger,
With a store of ale too, and thus ye must do
To make the wassail a swinger.

Give then to the king
And queen, wassailing:
And though with Ale ye be whet here,
Yet part ye from hence, as free from offence,
As when ye innocent met here.

*Distaff's Day was the day after Twelfth Night, when the women went
back to their work (to their distaff or spinning). The men went on
Plough Monday, which was the first Monday after Twelfth Night, giving
them, except where Twelfth Night fell on a Sunday, a longer holiday
than the women!*

ST DISTAFF'S DAY

Partly work and partly play
Ye must on St Distaff's Day:
From the plough soon free your team,
Then come home and fodder them.
If the maids a spinning go,
Burn the flax and fire the tow;
Scorch their plackets, but beware
That ye singe no maidenhaire
Bring in pails of water then,
Let the maids bewash the men.
Give St Distaff all the right,
Then bid Christmas sport goodnight;
And next morrow, everyone,
To his own vocation.

*The end of the Christmas season was 2 February, Candlemas, when all
decorations must come down for fear of the spirits trapped in the
evergreen boughs wreaking havoc.*

CEREMONIES UPON CANDLEMAS EVE

Down with the Rosemary, and so
Down with the Bays and Mistletoe;
Down with the Holly, Ivy, all,
Wherewith ye drest the Christmas Hall:
That so the superstitious find
No one least branch left there behind:
For look, how many leaves there be
Neglected, there (maids, trust me)
So many goblins you shall see.

And finally for Candlemas Day:

Kindle the Christmas Brand, and then
Till sunset let it burn;
Which quench'd, then lay it up again
Till Christmas next return.

Ritual for the Christmas log (Wright & Stokes, c. 1910).

Part must be kept, wherewith to tend
The Christmas log next year,
And where 'tis safely kept, the fiend
Can do no mischief there.

Not Without Mustard

AN ANECDOTE BY BEN JONSON AT WILL SHAKESPEARE'S EXPENSE

Maria Hubert

S hakespeare's father, John, died a gentleman with his own arms thanks to the efforts of his son, William. He had longed for his own crest all his life and he died a happy and fulfilled man! He had been a small tenant farmer on the land of the wealthy Ardens, but managed to better himself by becoming a glovemaker and asking for the hand of Mary Arden, his lord's daughter. The dowry consisted of two farms, which enabled the ambitious John to better himself even further. It seems slightly odd that a great lord would grant his daughter's hand to a humble glovemaker, but perhaps the fact that both John Shakespeare and the Arden family were Roman Catholics assisted their union.

Of the eight children born to John and Mary, Will was the third eldest. They would have been brought up as Catholics at first and in 1569, when Will was just five, John became Bailiff of Stratford. So it is another odd fact that shortly after this period of wealth and acceptance, the Shakespeares began to lose their status rapidly.

At about this time there were fines imposed on those who wished to continue practising their old religion, but as long as they accepted the monarch as head of the Church in England they were allowed to continue. But the fines became higher and harder to meet and the impositions greater. The crime of harbouring a recusant priest, which many of the big families did, was punishable by death. Consequently, a much poorer John Shakespeare struggled to bring up his children and send them to the local grammar school, and Will's own studies were to be cut short by the severe financial problems of his father.

By 1576 John had lost one of his farms and mortgaged the other. His public standing had slipped and he lived very quietly. The children, at least outwardly, were educated conforming to the new English Catholic Church established by Henry VIII, but all hopes of a family coat of arms were lost.

John, however, had been an honest and upright citizen and never lost the respect of his fellows, and the final acquisition of arms through his son, William, made his life complete. The arms were a falcon holding a spear and the motto, *Non Sans Droict* – 'Not without Right'. William Shakespeare finally became the son of a gentleman, although his mother was already a lady. This fact caused ribaldry and amusement among his peers and his great friend Ben Jonson was among the loudest to tease. He did in fact write a comedy which had a man whose coat of arms was a parody of Shakespeare's. In it the arms showed a boar's head – representing Will no doubt – and the motto was 'Not without Mustard'! The Christmas boar's head always had a pot of mustard and so, according to Jonson, did Will Shakespeare have 'mustard' (cheek) to request the arms of her Majesty.

A Talk for Twelfth Night

Arthur Machen

Arthur Machen, 1863–1947, was a writer and an actor. In 1901 he joined the Shakespeare Repertory Company under Sir Frank Benson and later worked as a journalist on the London Evening News. *The following is an after-dinner talk given for a Twelfth Night dinner in which he refers to those middle years he spent in repertory.*

The chief passion of Shakespeare's life was Stratford-upon-Avon. He never forgot it. Amid all the wild whirl of that London life – and it was a wild whirl then, a foaming torrent of such passions, political, sensual, emotional, intellectual, that our poor attempts at being alive in London now are pretty much as the green stuff on a duck pond is to Niagara – he thought of the friendly fires and the good taverns and the solid, stolid, worthy people and the beloved fields. Romeo and Juliet, Hamlet, Othello – so many steps nearer to the haven where he would be, to the true, secure life he loved. We think our London a tremendous centre of excitement; we, who are impressed when someone takes hold of a revue which is a failure and turns it into a success. William Shakespeare lived in a London which was impressed when it saw live men disembowelled at Tyburn and the heads of traitor nobles spiked on London Bridge. He lived in a red hot world; a world of terrific beauty, horror, cruelty, disgust, revelry. Our tea-party

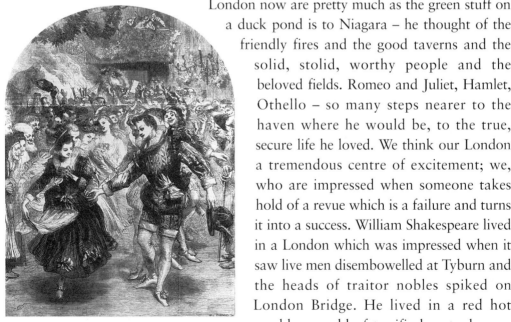

Christmas dancing at Queen Elizabeth I's court, from W. Sandys' Christmastide *(1830).*

people and commentating Dons do not begin to have the elementary data – as they would say – for the understanding of Shakespeare. I do not believe many of them have read Ben Jonson's description of a voyage down Fleet Ditch; they had better not, it would make them unwell . . .

To the horrible people who are best designated as Dons, whose idea of Heaven is an everlasting examination, it is repulsive that this young wastrel, with a possible Grammar School smattering, should have written the finest things in the world. 'The Warwickshire yokel', says one of them, in high contempt. And so has arisen the most marvellous folly of the world: the Baconian Hypothesis. Grave men, first being assured that shabby bohemian fellows do not write immortalities, have committed themselves to the wonderful lunacies of the Bilateral Cypher, have gone a little farther, and have at last found that Bacon wrote not only all Shakespeare but all the literature of his age, including Montaigne's *Essais* and Cervantes' *Quixote*. The last book which I read on the subject showed that *Don Quixote* should be read 'd'un qui s'ote' concerning one who hides himself – Bacon, of course. Indeed the writer proved that the alleged author, Cervantes, had an illegitimate child and was very poor: which is evidence, of course, that he could not write masterpieces! The masterpieces are notoriously written by mortal men with large banking accounts.

May this January, this Twelfth Night, bring us better sense, as we sit about our sea-coal fire.

Twelfth Day Feasts at Hampton Court

From the diaries and papers of Sir Dudley Carleton, 1604–7

In the early days of James I many Christmases were held at Hampton Court. Inigo Jones was by this time the favoured writer of the royal

Christmas entertainment. His masques were elaborate, depending on expensive scenery and special effects, rather than on the excellence of wit and words of Shakespeare's plays, though many were full of topical jokes and innuendos. An important part of the festivities were the card games and at court the nobles, whom Elizabeth had tried hard to send home to their country estates for Christmas, played over vast sums of money getting themselves and their estates into often irrevocable debt, as can be seen from the following accounts.

Twelfth Day 1604

The Twelfth Day the French Ambassador was feasted publicly, and at night there was a play in the Queen's presence, with a masquerade of certain scotchmen; who came in with a sword dance, not unlike a matachin; and performed it cleanly; from whence the King went to dice, into his own presence, and lost 500 crowns which marred a gamester; for since he appeared not there but once before was it at in the same place and parted a winner. The Sunday following was the greete day of the Queene's masque, at which was present the Spanish and Polack ambassadors with their whole trains, and the most part of the Florentines and the Savoyards, but not the ambassadors themselves, who were in strong competition for place and precedence, that to displease neither it was thought best to let both alone.

January 8th 1607

On the Twelfth Eve there was a greate Golden play at Court. No Gamester admitted that brought not £300 at least. Montgomery played the King's money, and won him £750, which he had for his labour. The Lord Montegle lost the Queen £400, Sir Robert Cary, for the Prince, £300, and the Earl Salisbury, £300; the Lord Buckhurst, £500; *et sic coeteris.* So that I heard of no winner but the King and Sir Francis Wolley, who got about £800. The King went a Hawking-journey yesterday to Theobalds and returns tomorrow.

Above Westminster the Thames is quite frozen over; and the Archbishop came from Lambeth, on Twelfth-day, over the ice to Court. Many fanciful experiments are daily put in practice; as certain youths burnt a gallon of wine upon the ice, and made all the passengers partakers. But the best is, of an honest woman (they say) that had a great longing to encrease her family on the Thames!

John Chamberlaine, in a letter to Sir Dudley Carleton.

The Boar's Head Carol and The Christmas Prince

AN ACCOUNT OF AN ELIZABETHAN CUSTOM

William Sandys

Of the many known carols which refer to the noble meal, the following is the original one from the Elizabethan era. It was first sung before the Prince of Christmas at John the Baptist's College, Oxford during the festivities in 1607. A numerous court (of players) was appointed and the 'Prince', one Mr Thomas Tucker, with plays and pageants and entertainments continuing well past Christmas until Shrovetide.

It should be explained here that it was the custom throughout the land to elect a Prince for the season of Christmas, who would rule over the revels. His word was law. Christmas lasted much longer then than it does now, and frequently surpassed Twelfth Night and carried on until the feast of the Purification, Candlemas, on 2 February. Shrove Tuesday, what we now call Pancake Tuesday, was the end of feasting, for the next day began the long Lenten Fast of the Church in preparation for Easter. An account from The Christmas Prince, *reprinted by William Sandys in 1833, tells of the meal:*

The first messe was a boar's head, which was carried in by ye tallest and lustiest of all ye guard, before whom (as attendants) wente first, one attired in a horesman's coat, with a boars speare in his hande, next to him an other huntsman in greene, with a bloody faucion drawne; next to him 2 pages in tafatye sarcenet, each of yem with a messe of mustard; next to whome came hee it carried ye boares-head crost with a greene silke scarfe, by which hunge ye empty scabbard of ye faulcion, which was carried before him. As he entered ye hall, he sang this Christmas Caroll, ye three last verses of euerie staffe being repeated after him by ye whole companye.

'*The boar is dead lo, here is his head*' (*Walter Crane, 1870*).

The Boar is dead,
Lo, here is his head:
What man could have done more
Than his head off to strike,
Meleanger like,
And bring it as I do before?

The living spoiled
Where good men toiled,
Which makes kind Ceres sorry;
But now dead and drawn,
Is very good brawn
And we have brought it for ye.

Then set down the swineyard,
The foe to the vineyard,
Let Bacchus crown his fall;
Let this boar's head and mustard
Stand for pig, goose and custard,
And so you are welcome all.

The Old and Young Courtier

AN ANONYMOUS RHYME, THE COMPLETE TEXT GLEANED FROM PEPYS, PERCY'S RELIQUES AND VITZELLY

This is a topical rhyming story from the seventeenth century, which has appeared in many collections from Pepys to the Percy Reliques *to* Vitzelly. *No one seems to know where it originated or who wrote it, but it is typical of the ballads sung for entertainment at Christmas events, and it describes the differences between life in the time of a courtier at Queen Elizabeth's Court with that of one at the Court of King James, spanning Shakespeare's own lifetime and changes perfectly. The queen was opposed to the fashion, then prevalent, of country gentlemen spending Christmas in London; and a letter of the period written by her orders 'The gentlemen of Norfolk and Suffolk are commanded to depart from London before Christmas, and repair to their counties, and there to keep hospitality among their neighbours.' The country gentry, however, appear to have availed themselves of the opportunity of gratifying their hankering for town life when there was no imperious queen to issue her opposing commands, for we find a writer from the reign of James I expressing himself in the following way:*

Much do I detest that effeminacy of the most that burn out day and night in their beds, and by the fireside in trifles, gaming, or courting their yellow mistresses all the winter in the city; appearing, but as cuckoos in the spring, one time in the year to the country and their tenants, leaving the care of keeping good houses at Christmas to the honest yeoman of the country.

Chorus
I'll sing you a song, made by a fine old pate,
Of a worshipful old gentleman, who had a great estate,
That kept a great old house at a bountiful rate,
And an old porter to relieve the poor at his gate:
Like an old Courtier of the Queen's
And the Queen's old Courtier.

With an old lady, who anger one word assuages,
That every quarter paid their servants their wages,
And never kept what belonged to coachman, footman nor pages,
But kept twenty old fellows with blue coats and badges:
Chorus

With an old study filled full of learned old books,
With an old reverend chaplain, you might know him by his looks,
With a buttery hatch worn quite off the hooks,
And an old kitchen, that maintained half a dozen old cooks:
Chorus

With an old hall, hung about with pikes, guns and bows,
With old swords and bucklers, that had borne many shrewd blows,
And an old frieze coat, to cover his worship's trunk hose,
And a cup of old sherry, to comfort his copper nose:
Chorus

With a good old fashion, when Christmas was come,
To call in all his old neighbours with bagpipe and drum,
With good cheer enough to furnish every old room,
And an old liquor able to make a cat speak, and man dumb;
Chorus

With an old falconer, huntsman, and a kennel of hounds,
That never hawked, nor hunted, but in his own grounds;
Who, like a wise man, kept himself within his own bounds,
And when he died gave every child a good thousand pounds:
Chorus

But to his eldest son his house and land he assigned,
Charging him in his will to keep the old bountiful mind,
To be good to his old tenants, and to his neighbours be kind,
But in the ensuing ditty you shall hear how he was inclined:
Like a young courtier of the King's,
And the King's young courtier.

Like a flourishing young gallant, newly come to his land,
Who keeps a brace of painted Madams at his command,
And takes up a thousand pounds upon his father's land,*
And gets drunk in a tavern, till he can neither go nor stand:
Chorus

With a new-fangled lady that is dainty, nice and spare,
Who never knew what belonged to good housekeeping, or care,
Who buys gaudy coloured fans to play with wanton air,
And seven or eight dressings** of other women's hair:
Chorus

With a new-fashioned hall, built where the old one stood,
Hung round with new pictures, that do the poor no good,
With a fine marble chimney, wherein burns neither coal nor wood,
And a new smooth shovelboard, whereon no victuals e'er stood:
Chorus

With a new study stuft full of pamphlets and plays,
And a new chaplain that swears faster than he prays,
With a new buttery hatch, that opens once in four or five days,
And a new French cook, to devise fine kickshaws and toys:
Chorus

With a new fashion, when Christmas is drawing on,
On a new journey to London straight we all must begone,

* A loan
** A wig

And leave none to keep house, but our new porter, John,
Who relieves the poor with a thump on the back with a stone.
Chorus

With a new gentleman usher, whose carriage is complete,
With a new coachman, footmen, and pages to carry up the meat,
With a waiting-gentlewoman, whose dressing is very neat,
Who, when her lady has dined, lets the servants not eat:
Chorus

With new titles of honour bought with his father's old gold,
For which sundry of his ancestor's old manors are sold.
And this is the course most of our new gallants hold,
Which makes that good housekeeping is now grown so cold,
Among the young courtiers of the King,
Or the King's young courtiers.

Christmas at the Inns of Court

AN EXTRACT FROM CUSTOMS AND CAROLS

William Sandys

*The custom of acting plays at court, at the City School of Westminster
and at the Inns of Court was well established by Elizabeth's reign, and
the year Shakespeare was born, the boys of Westminster School put on a
performance called* Truth, Faithfulnesse & Mercye. *The Christmas
Historian William Sandys takes up the story:*

Masques and pageants were in great request as well as plays, and the
Inns of Court vied with each other in the magnificence of their revels.

Christmas procession at the Inns of Court, from Dawson's Christmas and its Associations
(1909).

In the 4th year of Elizabeth, there was a splendid Christmas kept at the Inner Temple, wherin Lord Dudley was the chief person, Constable & Marshall under the name Palaphilos, and Christopher Hatton (afterwards Chancellor) was Master of the Game. Previous to this, a sort of parliament was held on St Thomas' eve, to decide whether they should keep it, and if so, to publish the officers' names, and then, 'in token of joy and good liking, the bench and company pass beneath the hearth and sing a carol, and so to boyer'.

At these grand Christmases there were revels and dancing during the twelve days of Christmas. It was about this time that 'Ferrex and Porrex' was acted before the Queen by the gentlemen of the Inner Temple; the printer stating it to be 'for furniture of part of the grande Christmas in the Inner Temple'. The order of the usual Christmas amusements at the inns of Court of this period would cause some curious scenes if carried into effect in the present day. Barristers singing and dancing before the judges, serjeants, and benchers would 'draw a house' if spectators were admitted. Of so serious import was this dancing considered, that, by an order in Lincoln's Inn, of February 7th, James I under the barristers were by decimation put out of commons, because the whole bar offended by not dancing on Candlemas day preceding, according to the ancient order of the society, when the judges were present: with a threat that if the fault were repeated, they should be fined or disbarred. Dugdale gives the following description of the Inner Temple revels, the three grand days being All-Halloween, Candlemass, and Ascension Day.

> First the solemn Revells (after dinner and the play ended) are begun by the whole House, Judges, Serjeants at Law, Benchers; the Utter and Inner Bar; and they led by the Master of Revells: and one of the Gentlemen of the Utter Barr are chosen to sing a song to the Judges, Serjeants or Masters of the Bench, which is usually performed; and in default thereof, there may be an amerciement. Then the Judges and the Benchers take their places, and sit down at the upper end of the Hall. Which done, the Utter-Barristers, and Inner-Barristers, perform a second solemn Revell before them. Which ended, the Utter-Barristers take their places and sit down. Some of the Gentlemen of the Inner-Barr, do present the House with dancing, which is called the Post-revells, and continue their Dances, till the Judges or Bench think meet to rise and depart.

In 1594 there was a celebrated Christmas at Grey's Inn, of which an account was published under the title of *Gesta Grayorum*, so called in consequence of the great popularity at that time of the *Gesta Romanorum*. The entertainments appear to have been heavy and pedantic in their nature, though suited to the style of the age. The concluding performance was a Masque before the Queen at Shrovetide containing much of that flattery which prevailed in all exhibitions before her. She was so much pleased with the performance, that on the courtiers dancing a measure after the Masque was ended, she exclaimed, 'What! Shall we have bread and cheese after a Banquet?' Mr Henry Helmes was the prince chosen, who assumed the following style, and had a numerous court to support him.

'The High and Mighty Prince Henry Prince of Purpoole, Arch-Duke of Stapulia de Bernardina, Duke of High and Nether Holborn, Marquis of St Giles and Tottenham, Court Palatine of Bloomsbury and Clerkenwell, Great Lord of the Cantons of Islington, Kentish-Town, Paddington and

Knightsbridge, Knight of the most Heroical Order of the Helmet, and Sovereign of the same.'

These royal and public pageants lured many country gentlemen to the metropolis, who neglecting the comforts of their dependants in the country at this season, dissipated in town, part of their means for assisting them, and incapacitated themselves from continuing that hospitality for which the country had been so long noted. In order to check this practice, the gentlemen of Norfolk and Suffolk, were in 1589 commanded to depart for their countries, and there keep hospitality amongst their neighbours. The presence of the higher orders would have controlled the tendancy to drinking and riotous sports among the country people, which the resort of minstrels and other strollers at this time to taverns and ale-houses

Country gentlemen dissipate themselves in London, from W. Sandys' Christmastide *(1830).*

encouraged; while their real enjoyments would have been increased through the assistance and fostering care of their superiors.

Masques and plays with other Christmas festivities, continued throughout the reign of James I, and the Prince (Charles) himself occasionally performed and in particular gained great applause in Ben Jonson's Mask, *The Vision of Delight*, performed on Twelfth Night in 1617 when the Muscovy Ambassadors were entertained at Court.

On the Christmas Masque

A CRITIQUE OF BEN JONSON'S MASQUE OF CHRISTMAS

Laurence Whistler

Laurence, brother of Rex, made a serious study of English festivals and produced a short dissertation on the masque, which was popular in Shakespeare's England. An extract from this account is reproduced here.

It was then (in the time of Henry VIII) that the name 'Masque' was given to a form of revel that would become, in time, the most beautiful ever contrived for an English Christmas.

Like the Orders of Architecture, the Masque came to us from Italy, and was grafted into a native tradition. There was no need to introduce fancy dress, dancing and pageantry to England: at King Henry's first Christmas the 'disguisings' had cost no less that £584. But the Court had taken no active part until 1513 . . . The Court ladies lost their shyness in time, and immensely enjoyed dressing up for the Masque. Though Queen Elizabeth did not care to take the floor herself . . .

With Ben Jonson to provide the words and Inigo Jones the machinery and costumes, the masques of the Stuart Court were in good hands – so long as the poet's taste and scholarship were dominant; for the poet kept all in proportion, verse, song, dance and architecture. To the greatest of English Architects the first three merely provided a grand excuse for the fourth.

The collaboration began with 'The Masque of Blackness' performed on Twelfth Night, 1605. In the old England, the festival was not an affair of one day, but of twelve – the Twelve Days of Christmas – and Shakespeare's *Twelfth Night* had been eminently a Christmas diversion, with a strong flavour of seasonable Misrule. Inigo Jones returned from Italy full of scenic splendours, but he attempted no extravagance at first . . .

Year after year poet and architect explored the possibilities of Masquing. Thus in Hue and Cry after Cupid Inigo Jones introduced the *scena ductilis*, in the form of a great red cliff rising between two richly trophied pillars . . . Thus again, at the royal wish, Ben Jonson introduced the Antimasque of the grotesque and clownish characters to act as foil (to the beautiful and splendid).

In Christmas, his Masque, such characters appear by themselves. It is a minor work quite outside the grand tradition, yet not without the genial charm, and for all its drowsy jokes it does give a lively impression of Father Christmas, the figure he cut in the 17th century, before anyone in England had ever heard of Santa Claus.

With The Tempus and Comus in mind, it seems ingenuous to add that good poets other than Ben Jonson were writing for the festivals and entertainments of the age. In the Lord's Masque of 1613 Thomas Campion made the stars dance on earth to celebrate the nuptials of Princess Elizabeth. The last Masque before the Civil War was Inigo Jones' Salmacida Spolia – first under the brown fog of Calvinism. And yet, to believe that the Puritans really destroyed Christmas is like believing (and many do) that Dickens or the Prince Consort invented it!

Christmas lives! Loses one habit, acquires another, sometimes falls back into ancient ways – but lives.

The Masque of Christmas

Ben Jonson

Ben Jonson was playwright to Queen Elizabeth I and then James I. He and Shakespeare knew one another, and were often in the same location as they strove to please their majesties at court. In 1616, the year in which Shakespeare died, Jonson wrote and presented to the court of King James the most well known of all his works, The Masque of Christmas. *An elaborate play, with costumes designed by Inigo Jones, this led the way for the great Twelfth Night costume balls which were enjoyed for the next three hundred years.*

Presenting a Christmas entertainment at the court of King James I, from W. Sandys'
Christmastide *(1830).*

His characters each represented one of the elements of Christmas, personified. This being early post-Reformation days, one needed to be politically correct to survive. Thus references to 'Pope's-head-lane' refer to the old Roman Catholic religion which was not welcomed at court; also the reference to 'Friday-street' relates to the Catholic custom of the Friday fastday and abstinence from meat dishes. In order to be welcomed, Christmas is obviously anxious to show that, although his origins are in the old religion, he has moved with the times. The comic character of the old woman, Venus, exhibits the characteristics of the modern pantomime dame.

Directions
The Court being seated.
Enter CHRISTMAS *with two or three of the guard, attired in round Hose, long Stockings, a close Doublet, a high-crown'd Hat, with a Broach, a long thin beard, a Truncheon, little Ruffes, white Shoos, his Scarffes, and Garters tyed crosse, and his Drum beaten before him.*

Why, Gentlemen, doe you know what you doe? Ha! would you ha' kept me out? CHRISTMAS old Christmas, Christmas of London, and Capitayne Christmas? Pray you, let me be brought before my Ld. Chamberlayn. I'le not be answered else: Tis merry in hall when beards wag all: I ha' seen the time you ha' wish'd for me, for a merry Christmas; and now you ha' me, they would not let me in; I must come another time! a good jeast, as if I could come more than once a yeare; why I am no dangerous person, and so I told my friends o' the Guard. I am old Gregorie Christmas still, and though I come out of Pope's-head-alley, as good a protestant as any i' my Parish. The troth is, I ha' brought a Masque here, out o' the Citie, o' my own making, and doe present it by a sett of my Sonnes, that come out of the Lanes of London, good dancing Boyes all. It was intended, I confesse, for Curryers Hall; but because the weather has beene open, and the Livory not at leisure to see it till a Frost came, that they cannot worke, I thought it convenient, with some little Alterations, and the Groome o' the Revells hand to 't, to fit it for a higher Place; which I have done, and though I say it, another Manner of Device than your Newyeares night. Bones o' Bread, the King! (seeing his Mjty) Son Rowland! son Clem! be readie there in a trice: quick Boyes!

Enter his sons and daughters (ten in Number) led in, in a string, by CUPID who is attired in a flat capp, and a Prentice's coat, with Wings at his shoulders.

MISRULE in a Velvet Capp, with a sprigge, a short Cloke, great yellow ruffe (like a Reveller); his Torche-bearer bearing a Rope, a Cheese, and a Baskett.

CAROL, a long Tawny Coat, with a redd Capp, and a Flute at his Girdle; his Torche-bearer carrying a Song-booke open.

MINCED-PYE, like a fine Cook's wife, drest neat; her Man carrying a Pye, Dish and Spoones.

GAMBOL, like a Tumbler, with a Hoope and Bells; his Torche-bearer armed with a Colt-staff and a Binding-Cloth.

POST AND PAIR, with a Pair-royal of Aces in his Hat; his Garment all done over with Pairs and Purs; his Squire carrying a Boxe, Cards, and Counters.

NEW YEARE'S GIFT, in a blue coat, serving-man-like, with an Orange, and a Sprigge of Rosemary gilt on his head, his Hat full of Brooches, with a collar of Gingerbread; his Torche-bearer carrying a March-Pane with a Bottle of Wine on either arme.

MUMMING in a masquing pied suit, with a Vizard; her page bearing a browne Bowle, drest with Ribbands, and a Rosemary before her.

OFFERING, in a short Gowne, with a Porter's Staffe in his Hand, a Wyth borne before him, and a Bason, by his Torche-bearer.

BABY-CAKE drest like a Boy, in a fine long Coat, Biggin-bib, Muck-ender, and a little Dagger; his Usher bearing a great Cake, with a Beane and Pease.

They enter singing.

Now God preserve, as you well doe deserve,
Your Majesties all two there;

Your Highnesse small, with my good Lords all,
And, Ladies, how doe you there?

Give me leave to ask, for I bring you a Masque
From little, little, little London,
Which saye the King likes, I have passed the Pikes,
If not, Old Christmas is undone.

(*Noise without*)

CHR. A' peace, what's the matter there?

GAMB. Here's one o'Friday-street would come in.

CHR. By no meanes, nor out of neither of the Fish-streets, admit not man; they are not Christmas creatures: Fish, and Fasting dayes, foe! Sonnes, say'd I well? looke to 't.

GAMB. No bodie out o' Friday-street, nor the two Fish-streets there; doe yo' heare?

CAROL. Shall John Butter o' Milke-street come in? aske him.

GAMB. Yes, he may slip in for a Torche-bearer, so he melt not too fast, that he wil; I last till the Masque be done.

CHR. Right, Sonne.

Sings agen

Our Dances freight, is a matter of eight,
and two, the which are Wenches;
In all they be ten, foure Cockes to a Hen,
and will swim to the tune like Tenches.
Each hath his Knight, for to carry his light,
Which some would say are torches;
To bring them here, and to lead them there,

and home again in their owne porches.
Now their intent –

Enter VENUS, a deafe Tire-woman

VEN. Now all the Lordes blesse me, where am I, tro? where is Cupid? Serve the King? they may serve the Cobler well enough, some of 'em, for any courtesie they have, y'wisse; they ha' need o' mending; unrude people they are, your Courtiers, here was thrust upon thrust indeed! was it ever so hard to get in before, tro?

CHR. How now? what's the matter?

VEN. A place, forsooth, I do want a place; I would have a good place to see my Child act in before the King, and the Queenes Majesties (God blesse 'em) to night.

CHR. Why, here is no place for you.

Old Christmas and his children (R. Seymour, 1836).

VEN. Right forsooth, I am Cupid's Mother, Cupid's own Mother, forsooth; yes forsooth; I dwell in Pudding-lane; ay, forsooth, he is Prentise in Lovelane with a Bugle-maker,* that makes your Bobs, and Bird-bolts for Ladies.

CHR. Good Lady Venus of Pudding-lane, you must go out for all this.

VEN. Yes, forsooth, I can sit any where, so I may see my Cupid act; hee is a pretty Child, though I say it

---

* A buglemaker is a maker of glass beads.

that perhaps should not, you will say; I had him by my first Husband. He was a Smith forsooth, we dwelt in Doelittle-lane then, he came a moneth before his time, and that may make him somewhat imperfect; but I was a Fishmonger's daughter.

CHR. No matter for your Pedigree, your house; good Venus, will you depart?

VEN. Ay, forsooth, he'le say his part, I warrent him, as well as ere a Play boy of 'em all; I could ha' had money enough for him, an I would ha' been tempted, and ha' let him out by the weeke, to the King's Players; Master Burbadge has been about and about with me; and so has old Mr. Hemings too, they ha' need of him, where is he tro'a? I would faine see him, pray God they have given him some drinke since he came.

CHR. Are you ready Boyes? strike up, nothing will drown this noisesome dame but a Drum: a' peace, yet, I ha' not done. SING –
Now, their intent is about to present –

CAROL. Why, here be halfe of the properties forgotten, Father.

OFFERING. Post and Pair wants his pur-chops and his pur-dogs.

CAROL. Ha' you nere a Son at the Groom-Porters to beg or borrow a paire of Cards quickly?

GAMB. It shall not need, heer's your Son Cheater without, has Cards in his pocket.

OFFERING. Odds so; speake to the Guard to let him in, under the name of a propertie.

GAMB. And heer's New-yeare's-gift ha's an Orenge, and Rosemarie, but not a clove to stick in't.

NEW-YEAR. Why let one go to the Spicery.

CHR. Fie, fie, fie; 'tis naught, it's naught, boyes.

VEN. Why, I have Cloves, it be cloves you want, I have cloves in my purse, I never go without one in my mouth.

CAROL. And Mumming has not his Vizard neither.

CHR. No matter, his owne face shall serve for a punishment, and 'tis bad enough; has Wassell her boule, and Minc'd-pie her spoones?

OFFERING. I, I; but Mis-rule doth not like his suite: he saies they Players have lent him one too little, on purpose, to disgrace him.

CHR. Let him hold his peace, and his disgrace will bee the lesse: what? shall wee proclaime where wee were furnisht? Mum! Mum! a' peace, be readie, good Boyes.

Sings agen

Now their intent, is above to present,
With all the appurtainements
A right Christmas, as, of old, it was,
To be gathered out of the dances.

Which they do bring, and afore the king,
The Queen, and Prince, as it were now,
Drawn here by love; who over and above,
Doth draw himself in the geer too.

(Here the drum and fife sounds and they march about once. In the second coming up, CHRISTMAS *proceeds to his Song.)*

Hum, drum, sauce for a coney;
No more of your martial music;
Even for the sake O' the next new stake
For there I do mean to use it.

And now to ye, who in place are to see
With roll and farthingale hoopèd,

I pray you know, though he want of his bow,
By the wings, that this is CUPID.

He might go back, for to cry 'What you lack?'
But that were not so witty:
His cap and coat are enough to note
That he is the Love o' the City.

And he leads on, though he now begone,
For that was his only rule:
But now comes in Tom of Bosoms-Inn,
And he present-eth MISRULE.

Which you may know, by the very show,
Albeit you never ask it:
For there you may see what his ensigns be,
The rope, the cheese and the basket.

This CAROL plays, and has been in his days
A chirping boy, and a kill-pot.
Kit cobler it is, I'm a father of his,
And he dwells in the lane called Fill-pot.

But how is this? O my daughter Cis,
MINCED-PIE, with her do not dally
On pain o' your life; she's an honest cook's wife,
And comes out of Scalding-Alley.

Next in the trace, comes GAMBOL in place,
And to make my tale the shorter,
My son, Hercules, tane out of Distaff Lane,
But an active man, and a porter.

Now POST & PAIR, old Christmas's heir,
Doth make and a gingling sally;
And wot you who, tis one of my two
Sons, card-makers in Purr-alley.

Next, in a trice, with his box and his dice
Mac' pipin my son, but younger,
Brings MUMMING in; and the knave will win,
For he is a coster-monger.

But NEW-YEAR'S GIFT, of himself makes shift
To tell you what his name is;
With orange on head, and his gingerbread,
Clem Waspe, of Honey lane 'tis.

This, I tell you, is our jolly WASSEL,
And for Twelfth Night more meet too;
She works by the ell, and her name is Nell,
And she dwells in Threadneedle Street too.

Then OFFERING, he, with his dish and his tree,
That in every great house keepeth,
Is by my son, young Littleworth, done,
And in Penny-Rich Street sleepeth.

Last BABY-CAKE, that an end doth make
Of Christmas merry, Christmas vein-a,
Is child Rowlan, and a straight young man,
Though he comes out of crooked Lane-a.

There should have been, and a dozen, I ween,
But I could find but one more
Child of Christmas, and a LOG it was,
When I had them all gone o'er.

I prayed him, in a tune so trim,
That he would make one to prance it:
And I myself, would have been the Twelfth,
O! but LOG was too heavy to dance it.

Now Cupid, come you on.

CUPID. You worthie wights, King, Lordes and Knights,
O Queen, and Ladies bright:
Cupid invites you to the sights
He shall present to night.

VEN. 'Tis a good child, speake out, hold up your head, love.

CUPID. And which Cupid . . . And which Cupid . . .

VEN. Do not shake so Robin, if thou beest a-cold, I ha' some warme waters
for thee here.

CHR. Come, you put Robin Cupid out, with your waters, and your fisling;
will you be gone?

VEN. I forsooth, he's a child, you must conceive, and must be us'd tenderly;
he was never in such an assembly before, forsooth, but once at the Warmoll
Quest, forsooth, where he said grace as prettily as any of the Sheriffes
Hinchboyes, forsooth.

CHR. WILL YOU PEACE, FORSOOTH?

VEN. I, that's a good boy, speake plaine, Robin; how does his Majestie like
him, I pray? will he give him eight pence a day thinke you? Speake out
Robin.

CHR. Nay, he is out enough, you may take him away, and begin your
Dance; this is to have speeches.

VEN. You wrong the Child, you doe wrong the Infant, I 'peale to his
Majestie.

Here they dance.

CHR. Well done, Boyes, my fine Boyes, my Bully Boyes.

Sings agen

THE EPILOGUE

Nor doe you think their legges is all
the commendation of my Sons,
For at the Artillery-Garden they shall
as well (forsooth), use their Guns.

And march as fine, as the Muses nine,
along the streets of London:
And i' their brave tires, to gi' their false fires,
especially Tom, my Son.

Now if the lanes and the alleys afford
such an activity as this;
At Christmas next, if they keep their word
can the Children of Cheapside miss?

Tho', put the case, when they come in place,
they should not dance, but hop;
Their very gold lace, with their silk would 'em grace,
having so many knights o' the shop.

But were I so wise, I might seem to advise
so greate a potentate as yourselfe;
They should, sir, I tell 'e, spar't out of their belly
and this way spend some of their pelf.

Ay, and come to the Court, for to make you some Sport,
at leaste once every yeare:
As Christmas hath done, with his seventh or eighth Son,
and his couple of Daughters deare.

THE END

> *Many of the quips and references here are topical, the addresses local*
> *and, no doubt, some of the references have a double meaning and a*

bawdy intent. The whole introduction would be interspersed with much laughter from the audience, as the 'children' pranced and mimed to the rhyming introductions from their 'father', Christmas, who tried hard to get his acts together literally while Venus continued her devastating interruptions. From this play it may be seen that the early Jacobean audience, such as Shakespeare was writing for, would have been as much at home with the frivolous pantomime season as we are today.

An engraving of the coming of Father Christmas and his entourage at the court of King James I, c. 1820 (private collection).

'A Christmas Carroll'

THE CHRISTMAS SEASON IN VERSE

George Wither

George Wither was a poet born in Hampshire in 1588. The son of a country gentleman, he went to Oxford to study the classics until family financial problems, brought about by the fines paid to the Crown by all recusant Catholics at that time, meant that George had to go home and tend the plough. This task did not suit him and he quickly escaped to London where he sought to make his fortune at the royal court.

Disenchanted with court life, he was sent to prison for writing satirical poems about the life there and while in prison wrote some of his best pieces including Juvenilia, *from which the following poem comes. It describes vividly the Christmas experienced in the late sixteenth century, although some of the references are not immediately obvious. Verse 5 tells us that the poor man who pawns his rings and clothing all year retrieves them for Christmas, while the barmaid has been saving up by scraping the dregs from the beer barrels to sell for her own pennies. Verse 7 strikes at the matter close to Queen Elizabeth's heart, that of the landlords staying in London instead of going home to their estates and looking after their tenants. This task fell to the home farmers, who kept up the tradition of giving the workers and farm labourers a joint of meat, and a pie or cake. Verse 10 speaks of many old customs – the 'wenches with their wassail bowls' are of course the Vessel maidens from ancient times, who survived into living memory in parts of Britain. The 'Wild Mare' is another remnant of pagan belief, carried on in the Welsh 'Mari Lwyd', and the kitchen boy's broken box is the clay money box which servants made to collect their Christmas gift from their employers, hence 'Christmas Box' meaning a gift and 'Boxing Day' meaning the day when servants went around to collect their money. Verse 11 refers to the customs of Twelfth Night, when a King and Queen were chosen to rule the revels and master and servant changed places, sometimes called the 'Topsy-Turvy' feast.*

1

So, now is come our joyful'st feast;
Let every man be jolly.
Each room with Ivy-leaves is dress'd
And every post with holly.
Though some churls at our mirth repine,
Round your foreheads garlands twine,
Drown a sorrow in a cup of wine,
And let us all be merry.

2

Now all our neighbour's chimneys smoke,
And Christmas blocks are burning;
Their ovens they with baked meats choke,
And all their spits are turning.
Without the door let sorrow lie,
And if for cold it hap to die,
We'll bury't in a Christmas Pie,
And evermore be merry.

Loe this is he whose infant Muse began
To braue the World before yeares still'd him Man;
Though praise he sleight & scornes to make his Rymes
Begg fauors or opinion of the Tymes,
Yet few by good men haue bine more approu'd
None so unseene, so generally lou'd

Engraving of the seventeenth-century effigy of George Wither.

'Bag pipe, tabour and good gossip', from 'A Christmas Carroll' (illustration by Frank Merrill, 1895).

3

Now every lad is wondrous trim,
And no man minds his labour;
Our lasses have provided them
A bagpipe and a tabour.
Young men, and maids, and girls and boys,
Give life to one another's joys,
And you anon shall by their noise
Perceive that they are merry.

4

Rank misers now do sparing shun,
Their hall of music soundeth;
And dogs thence with whole shoulders run,
So all things there aboundeth.
The country folk themselves advance,

For crowdy-mutton's come out of France;
And Jack shall pipe, and Jill shall dance,
And all the town be merry.

5

Ned Swash hath fetched his bands from pawn,
And all his best apparel;
Brisk Nell hath bought a Ruff of Lawn
With droppings of the Barrel;
And those that hardly all the year
Had bread to eat or rags to wear,
Will have both clothes and dainty fare,
And all the days be merry.

6

Now poor men to the Justices
With Capons make their arants,
And if they hap to fail of these
They plague them with their warrants.
But now they feed them with good cheer,
And what they want they take in beer,
For Christmas comes but once a year,
And then they shall be merry.

7

Good farmers in the country nurse
The poor, that else were undone.
Some landlords spend their money worse,
On lust and pride at London.
There the roysters they do play,
Drab and dice their land away,
Which may be ours another day;
And therefore let's be merry.

8

The client now his suit forbears,
The prisoner's heart is eased,

The vices of a London Christmas in Elizabeth I's day (Frank Merrill, 1895).

The debtor drinks away his cares,
And for the time is pleased.
Though others' purses be more fat,
Why should we pine or grieve for that?
Hang sorrow, care will kill a cat,
And therefore let's be merry.

9

Hark, how the wags abroad do call
Each other forth to rambling;
Anon you'll see them in the Hall,
For nuts and apples scrambling.
Hark, how the roofs with laughters sound!
Anon they'll think the house goes round,
For they the cellar's depth have found,
And there they will be merry.

10

The wenches with their Wassail bowls,
About the streets are singing,
The boys are come to catch the Owls,
The Wild Mare in is bringing.
Our kitchen boy hath broke his box,
And to the dealing of the Ox
The honest neighbours come by flocks
And here they will be merry.

11

Now Kings and Queens poor sheep-cotes have.
And mate with everybody;
The honest now may play the knave,
The wise men play at noddy.
Some youths will now a-mumming go,
Some others play at Rowland-Hoe,
And twenty other gameboys moe,
Because they will be merry.

12

Then wherefore in these merry days
Should we, I pray, be duller?
No; let us sing some roundelays
To make our mirth the fuller.
And, whilst thus inspir'd we sing,
Let all the streets with echoes ring;
Woods, and hills, and everything,
Bear witness we are merry.

The Christmas dinner – human and canine!
(Frank Merrill, 1895).

'To Shorten Winter's Sadness'

From Thomas Weelkes' Madrigals

To shorten winter's sadness
See where the nymphs with gladness
Disguised are all a-coming,
Right wantonly a-mumming.
    Fa-la

Whilst youthful sports are lasting,
To feasting turn our fasting;
With revels and with Wassails
Make grief and care our vassals.
    Fa-la

For youth it will beseemeth
That pleasure he esteemeth;
And sullen age is hated
That mirth would have abated.
    Fa-la

Elizabethan mummers, from Christmas with the Poets *by the Vitzelly Brothers (1840).*

Pepys on Twelfth Night

A critique by the Rt Hon. G. Russell

On 6 January 1662 that indefatigable playgoer Mr Pepys recorded in his diary: 'After dinner to the Duke's House, and there saw Twelfth Night *acted well, though it be but a silly play and not related at all to the name.'*

'After dinner at the Duke's house.'

The final court of literary appeal – the general consent of the cultivated caste in modern Europe – has not confirmed Pepys' sentence on the 'silly play'; but when he speaks of it as, 'not related at all to the name' he makes a palpable hit, or at least indicates a lost opportunity. John Downes, writing a century after the play was composed, says it 'was got up on purpose to be acted on Twelfth Night', and this fact, if fact it be, only makes it more tantalising that the plot, the action, and the characters should bear no relation to the title. Shakespeare is Catholic as sea is salt. Did not the word, 'Catholicism' suggest to Mathew Arnold's mind 'the pell-mell of all men and women in Shakespeares plays'? Shakespeare painted the daily life of a rich and free humanity, with the Mass, and all that the Mass represents, as its sun and centre. It is a permissible exercise of literary fancy and festivity which he might have woven round the traditional observance of Twelfth Night, when in a Baron's Hall and minstrel-gallery the mirth of Christmas reached its topmost and final note, but not till, in the Mass of the Epiphany, men had once again paid their homage to the story of the Star. *Vidimus stellam Ejus in Oriente, et venimus adorare Eum.*

But it is idle to speculate on what Shakespeare might have done. What he actually did had in it enough of wonder and astonishment to satisfy John Milton, and what satisfied Milton may well suffice for our less heroic age. Only the title, *Twelfth Night*, haunts and tantalises us, and sets us dreaming of the immortal music in which Shakespeare, had he so willed, might have told the story and meaning of the Star.

Shakespeare and Christmas (II)

Max Beerbohm

Sir Henry Maximilian Beerbohm, 1876–1956, essayist and critic, considered the Bard's lack of references to Christmas as most suspicious and reeking of a hatred for the festive season. However, some of his facts are contradicted: according to the Oxford Companion to English literature, *Anne Hathaway was only eight years senior to Shakespeare and as he was born in 1564 and married in 1582 he must have been eighteen and she twenty-six, not thirty-eight as Beerbohm suggests in this piece. The following extract is taken from* A Christmas Garland.

That Shakespeare hated Christmas – hated it with a venom utterly alien to the gentle heart in him – I take to be a proposition that establishes itself automatically. If there is one thing lucid-obvious in the Plays and Sonnets, it is Shakespeare's unconquerable loathing of Christmas. The professors deny it, however, or deny that it is proven. With these gentlemen I will deal faithfully. I will meet them on their own parched ground, making them fertilise it by shedding there the last drop of water that flows through their veins.

If you find in the works of a poet, whose instinct it is to write about everything under the sun, one obvious theme untouched, or touched hardly at all, then it is at least presumable that there was some good reason for that abstinence. Such a poet was Shakespeare. It was one of the divine frailties of his genius that he must ever be flying off at a tangent from his main theme to unpack his heart in words about some frivolous small irrelevance that had come into his head. If it could be shown that he never mentioned Christmas, we should have proof presumptive that he consciously avoided doing so. But if the fact is that he mentioned it now and then, but in grudging fashion, without one spark of illumination – he, the arch-illuminator of all things – then we have proof positive that he detested it.

I see Dryasdust thumbing his Concordance. Let my memory save him the trouble. I will reel him off the one passage in which Shakespeare spoke of Christmas in words that rise to the level of mediocrity.

> Some say that ever 'gainst that Season comes
> Wherein our Saviour's birth is celebrated,
> The bird of dawning singeth all night long:
> And then, they say, no spirit dare stir abroad;
> The nights are wholesome; then no planets strike,
> No fairy takes, nor witch hath power to charm,
> So hallowed and so gracious is the time.

So says Marcellus at Elsinore. This is the best our Shakespeare can vamp up for the birthday of the Man with whom he of all men had the most in common. And Dryasdust, eternally unable to distinguish chalk from cheese, throws up his hands in admiration of the marvellous poetry. If Dryasdust had written it, it would more than pass muster. But as coming from Shakespeare, how feeble-cold – aye, and sulky-sinister! The greatest praiser the world will ever know! – and all he can find in his heart to sing of Christmas is a stringing together of old women's superstitions!

Again and again he has painted Winter for us as it has never been painted since – never by Goethe even, though Goethe in more than one of the 'Winterlieder' touched the hem of his garment. There was every external reason why he should sing, as only he could have sung, of Christmas. The Queen set great store by it. She and her courtiers celebrated it year after year with lusty pious unction. And thus the ineradicable snob in Shakespeare had the most potent of all inducements to honour the feast with the full power that was in him. But he did not, because he would not. What is the key to the enigma?

For many years I hunted it vainly. The second time that I met Carlyle I tried to enlist his sympathy and aid. He sat pensive for a while and then said it seemed to him a 'goose-quest'. I replied, 'You have always a phrase for everything Tom, but always the wrong one.' He covered his face, and presently, peering at me through his gnarled fingers, said 'Mon, ye're recht.' I discussed the problem with Renan, with Emerson, with Disraeli, also with Cetewayo, poor Cetewayo, best and bravest of men, but intellectually a professor, like the rest of them. It was borne in on me that if I were to win the heart of the mystery I must win alone.

The solution, when it suddenly dawned on me, was so simple stark I was ashamed of the ingenious-clever ways I had been following. (I learned then – and perhaps it is the one lesson worth the learning of any man – that the truth may be approached only through the logic of the heart. For the heart is eye and ear, and all excellent understanding abides there.) On Christmas Day, assuredly, Anne Hathaway was born.

In what year she was born I do not know nor care. I take it she was not less than thirty-eight when she married Shakespeare. This however is sheer conjecture and in no way important-apt to our enquiry. It is not the year, but the day of the year that matters. All we need bear in mind is that on Christmas Day that woman was born into the world.

If there be any Doubting Thomas among my readers, let him not be afraid to utter himself. I am (with the possible exception of Shakespeare) the gentlest man that ever breathed, and I do but bid him study the plays inthe light I have given him. The first thing that will strike him is that Shakespeare's thoughts turn constantly to the birthdays of all his Fitton-heroines, as a lover's thoughts always do turn to the moment at which the loved one first saw the light. 'There was a star danced, and under that' . . . was born Beatrice. Juliet was born 'on Lammas Eve'. Marina tells us she derived her name from the chance of her having been 'born at seas'. And so on, throughout the whole gamut of women in whom Mary Fitton was bodied forth to us. But mark how carefully Shakespeare never says a word about the birthdays of the various shrews and sluts in whom, again and again, he gave us his wife. When and where was born Queen Constance the scold? And Bianca? And Doll Tearsheet, and 'Greasy Jane' in the song, and all the rest of them? It is of the last importance that we should know. Yet never a hint is vouchsafed us in the text. It is clear that Shakespeare cannot bring himself to write about Anne Hathaway's birthday – will not stain his imagination by thinking of it. That is entirely human-natural. But why should he loath Christmas Day itself with precisely the same loathing? There is but one answer – and that inevitable-final. The two days were one.

Some soul secrets are so terrible that the most hardened realist of us may well shrink from laying them bare. Such a soul-secret was this of Shakespeare's. Think of! The gentlest spirit that ever breathed, raging and fuming endlessly in impotent-bitter spleen against the prettiest of festivals! Here is a spectacle so tragic piteous that, try as we will, we shall not put it from us. And it is well that we should not, for in our pleniary compassion, we should but learn to love the man the more.

Christmas at the Mermaid

IN PRAISE OF THE BARD BY HIS FRIENDS

Theodore Watts-Dunton

Theodore Watts was born in 1832 and was a solicitor in his early life. He was to become one of the most influential writers for the Athenaeum and its chief poetry reviewer from 1876–1902. The following extract is a romantic whimsy from his book of the same title, published in 1902. It describes how, after Shakespeare has retired to Stratford, his friends meet at the Mermaid Inn one Christmas to reminisce. Ben Jonson, fellow playwright, holds the floor with an old rhyme used for rounds of Christmas story-telling. The Friend of Shakespeare then takes the floor to tell the story of Shakespeare as a child and grown up with his sweetheart. The Christmas rounds continue with other less happy tales. Watts changed his named to Watts-Dunton in 1896 and married a younger woman late in life (in 1905) and died in 1914.

With the exception of Shakespeare, who has quitted London for good in order to reside at New Place, Stratford-on-Avon, which he has lately rebuilt, all the members of the Mermaid Club are assembled at the Mermaid Tavern. At the head of the table sits Ben Jonson dealing out the Wassail from a large bowl. At the other end sits Raleigh, and at Raleigh's right hand the guest he has brought with him, a stranger called David Gwynn, the Welsh seaman who is now an elderly man. The story of his exploits as a galley slave in crippling the Armada before it reached the Channel had, years before, whether true or false, given him a great reputation in the Low Countries, the echo of which had reached England. Raleigh's desire was to excite the public enthusiasm for continuing the struggle with Spain on the sea and generally revive the fine Elizabethan temper, which had already become a thing of the past, save perhaps among such choice spirits as those associated with the Mermaid Club.

CHORUS
Christmas knows a merry, merry place,
Where he goes with fondest face,
Brightest eye, brightest hair:
Tell the Mermaid where is that one place:
        Where?

BEN JONSON
(After filling each cup with Wassail)
Drink first to Stratford Will – beloved man,
So generous, honest, open, brave and free,
Who merriest at the Apollo used to be –
Merriest of all the merry Falcon clan.

(All drink to Will Shakespeare)

CHORUS

BEN JONSON
That he, the star of revel, bright eyed Will,
With life at golden summit, fled the town
And took from Thames that light to dwindle down
O'er Stratford's farms, doth make me marvel still.

But tho' we feast without the king tonight,
The Monarch leaves a regent – friend of friends,
With whose own soul the thronèd spirit blends
In one fair flame of love's conmingling light.

Brother of Shakespeare, wilt thou not rehearse
Those sugared sonnets thy shy muse hath made,
Those lines where Avon, glassing wood and glade,
Seems rippling through the sunshine of thy verse?

Wilt thou not tell the Mermaid once again,
In golden numbers, what the poet told,
Of how his spirit ever was controlled
By Avon-ripples shining in his brain.

Christmas at the Mermaid Inn.

And how those ripples greeted him that day,
Which was the Mermaid's night, when he, the Swan
Flew to the bosom he was nursed upon –
The bosom he loved when far away?

Wilt thou not tell us how the river spake
To that sweet Swan returning to its nest
Among the lilies dreaming on the breast
Of Avon, dear to us for Shakespeare's sake?

CHORUS

SHAKESPEARE'S FRIEND
To sing the Nation's song, or do the deed
That crowns with richer light the Motherland,
Or lend her strength of arm in hour of need
When fangs of foes shine fierce on every hand,
Is joy to him whose joy is working well –
Is goal and guerdon too, though never fame
Should find a thrill of music in his name;
Yea, goal and guerdon too, though Scorn should aim
Her arrows at his soul's high citadel.

But if the fates withhold the joy from me
To do the deed that widens England's day
Or join the son of Freedom's jubilee
Begun when England started on her way –
Withhold from me the hero's glorious power
To strike with song or sword for her, the mother,
And give that sacred guerdon to another,
Him will I hail as my more noble brother –
Him will I love for his diviner dower.

Enough for me who have our Shakespeare's love
To see a poet win the poet's goal,
For Will is he; enough and far above
All other prizes to make rich my soul.
Ben names my numbers golden. Since they tell

A tale of him who in his peerless prime
Fled us ere yet one shadowy film of time
Could dim the lustre of that brow sublime,
Golden my numbers are: Ben praiseth well.

A FRIEND OF MARLOWE'S
(Who has been sitting moody and silent)
'Tis when the Christmas joy-bells fill the air
That memory comes with half reproachful eyes
To hold before the soul its legacies,
Of grief and joy from Christmas-songs that were.

Christmas knows a merry, merry place
Where he goes with fondest face,
Brightest eye, brightest hair:
Tell the Mermaid where is that one place:
Where?

WASSAIL CHORUS
CHORUS
Christmas knows a merry, merry place,
Where he goes with fondest face,
Brightest eye, brightest hair:
Tell the Mermaid where is that one place:
Where?

RALEIGH
'Tis by Devon's glorious halls,
Whence, dear Ben, I come again:
Bright with golden roofs and walls –
El Dorado's rare domain –
Seem those halls when sunlight launches
Shafts of gold through leafless branches,
Where the winter's feathery mantle blanches
Field and farm and lane.

CHORUS
Christmas knows a merry, merry place,
Where he goes with fondest face,

Brightest eye, brightest hair:
Tell the Mermaid where is that one place:
Where?

DRAYTON
'Tis where Avon's wood-sprites weave
Through the boughs a lace of rime,
While the bells of Christmas Eve
Fling for Will the Stratford-chime
O'er the river-flags embossed
Rich with flowery runes of frost –
O'er the meads where snowy tufts are tossed –
Strains of olden time.

CHORUS
Christmas knows a merry, merry place,
Where he goes with fondest face,
Brightest eye, brightest hair:
Tell the Mermaid where is that one place:
Where?

SHAKESPEARE'S FRIEND
'Tis, methinks, on any ground
Where our Shakespeare's feet are set.
There smiles Christmas, holly-crowned
With his blithest coronet:
Friendship's face he loveth well:
'Tis a countenance whose spell
Sheds a balm o'er every mead and dell
Where we used to fret.

CHORUS
Christmas knows a merry, merry place,
Where he goes with fondest face,
Brightest eye, brightest hair:
Tell the Mermaid where is that one place:
Where?

HEYWOOD
More than all the pictures, Ben,
Winter weaves by wood or stream,
Christmas loves our London, when
Rise thy clouds of wassail-steam –
Clouds like these, that, curling, take
Forms of faces gone, and wake
Many a lay from lips we loved, and make
London like a dream.

CHORUS
Christmas knows a merry, merry place,
Where he goes with fondest face,
Brightest eye, brightest hair:
Tell the Mermaid where is that one place:
Where?

BEN JONSON
Love's old songs shall never die,
Yet the new shall suffer proof;
Love's old drink of Yule brew I,
Wassail for new love's behoof:
Drink the drink I brew, and sing
Till the berried branches swing,
Till our song make all the Mermaid ring –
Yea, from rush to roof.

FINALE
Christmas loves this merry, merry place:
Christmas saith with fondest face
Brightest eye, brightest hair:
'Ben! the drink tastes rare of sack and mace:
Rare!'

ACKNOWLEDGEMENTS

The comments and eccentricities of some of the critics quoted in this book are not necessarily in accord with my own thoughts. The original grammar and spelling has been retained in most extracts and for this reason there may be inconsistencies.

Special acknowledgemant is to William Heinemann for permission to reproduce 'Shakespeare and Christmas' from *A Christmas Garland* by Max Beerbohm (1912). *The Masque of Christmas* by Ben Jonson is pieced together from two copies, *The Book of Christmas & New Yeare* (1860) and *Righte Merrie Christmasse* (1890). References are also made to the following: *Ben Jonson*, Herford and Percy (Oxford, 1925), *The Masque of Christmas*, Whistler (Curtain Press, n.d.), which uses the Carisbrook Library version of 1890, 'Dissitation on the Masques', Whistler from *The Masque of Christmas* (Curtain Press). 'Now Thrice Welcome Christmas' by George Wither is taken from *Poor Robins Kalendar* (n.d.). The accounts of the Grand Exhibition of the Christmas Prince at St John's College Oxford, 1607, were reproduced from a leaflet of that title, reprinted in 1816. The quote on a seventeenth-century Christmas dinner was taken from *The English Housewife* by Gervase Markham.

Research for 'Shakespearean Christmas Presents' included details from the following sources: W. Sandys, *Carols Old and New* (1833); *Nichols' Progresses* and *Illustrations of Manners & Expences* (1647); Roper, *Life of Sir Thomas Moore* (n.d.); W. Sandys, *Christmastide* (1830) and numerous others. The extract from Christmas at the Mermaid comes from Theodore Watts-Dunton's book, *Christmas at the Mermaid* (John Lane, 1902).

The illustrations are courtesy of the Christmas Archives Internaional.